Mark H. Maxwell is an entertainment attorney, music business veteran and college professor. As a lawyer, Mark represents a diverse roster of recording artists, celebrities, record labels, music publishers, authors, songwriters, and producers. As a professor in Belmont University's prestigious entertainment business and songwriting program, he created their popular course on Bob Dylan and teaches courses on music business, faith and culture, and copyright law. Mark is passionate about serving as a mentor to the next generation of creatives and entertainment business professionals. He lives in Nashville with his wife and children.

MARKHMAXWELL.COM

PRAISE FOR *NETWORKING KILLS: SUCCESS THROUGH SERVING*

"I knew I wanted to get my hands on Mark Maxwell's book, *Networking Kills*, when one of his Belmont students quoted it in a conversation we were having over a cup of coffee. What a simple concept: 'Networking' narrows our focus and our life experience. 'Serving' connects us in a meaningful way and throws the gates of opportunity wide open. Let the adventure begin!"
— **Amy Grant, Grammy award-winning singer/songwriter**

"I have had the privilege of knowing and working with Mark Maxwell for some time now. In an industry and culture that encourages us to be more and more self-focused for our own personal gain, Mark's book is a fresh and necessary perspective that is desperately needed. It is natural for us to think that our gifts and talents are for us. Mark does a great job of leading us through his book and turning this paradigm upside down. No matter where we are on the journey we need to constantly be reminded that we are called to serve not be served."
— **TobyMac, Grammy award-winning recording artist**

"Culture teaches us to measure everything through the question: 'how does this benefit my life?' This book does the exact opposite by changing the question to, 'how does my life benefit others?' Mark Maxwell's book, *Networking Kills*, is more than just a novel idea—this significant message can help steer a generation towards true success. But more than just this generation, I believe it will help anyone, in any stage, re-evaluate their motivations and navigate their life back to what truly matters. I know it's doing that for me."
— **Natalie Grant, award-winning recording artist**

"In his book, *Networking Kills*, Mark Maxwell shares a compelling message that disrupts our current culture of selfish ambition and self-promotion. His message of serving others is profound, not only because it's true, but because as my friend and counselor I've seen Mark live it out in his everyday life. His story and wisdom are instructional and inspirational!"
— **Gregg Dedrick - Former CEO of Kentucky Fried Chicken & Founder of Iron Bell Music**

"Mark Maxwell was an early believer and important counselor for MercyMe twenty years ago. I am thrilled that through his book, *Networking Kills*, he continues to authentically mentor and counsel the next generation concerning true success-- success that is only found through serving others."

—Bart Millard, MercyMe

"With *Networking Kills*, Mark Maxwell is seemingly flying in the face of what the assumed 'best approach' is for building a successful career in the music industry... network, network, network! When in reality, every person doing business—including us creatives—are all truly in the service industry. Mark's call to think about our roles in the context of service is refreshing and spot on. Kudos, Mr. Maxwell!"

— busbee, Grammy-nominated songwriter/producer (Lady Antebellum, P!nk, Keith Urban, Maren Morris, Jon Bellion, Carly Pearce)

"I am grateful Mark Maxwell is bringing this timely message to students everywhere. In *Networking Kills*, he dismantles the networking myth concerning success while illuminating the truth about finding true purpose in life. Serving is the key!"

— Judge Alberto R. Gonzales, former White House counsel & U.S. Attorney General; Dean of Belmont University College of Law

"The message in this book is a great reminder that when we focus on serving, we're really focusing on other people. And, as Mark writes: 'Networking has become a distraction and an inhibitor in the creative development process that will keep us from creating lasting works with deep impact on our culture.'"

— Zach Williams - Grammy award-winning singer/songwriter

"Mark Maxwell and his wife, Carol, have been longtime wonderful friends and encouragers of Newsong and Winter Jam! I was so encouraged and challenged by Mark's book, *Networking Kills*. I love Mark's heart for serving and allowing God to do the networking :) Telling His story is the ultimate act of serving."

— Eddie Carswell, Winter Jam Tour owner/founder

"I love Mark! His book, *Networking Kills*, is a timely reminder on the truth behind real connectivity and thriving relationship."

— Peter Furler, singer/songwriter/producer

"'Networking for success' is a topic covered everywhere, but it really takes a special person to understand how to capture the human element of it. Mark is one of the only people that could bring that element out with his book because he just IS that person in my own life. Much like the way the author lives his everyday life, Mark's book, *Networking Kills*, proves that the best way to navigate professionally is with a certain genuine kindness and authenticity. Calling on yourself to think about intentions and how service equals success and how you contribute to other's successes above all else is truly a mentally game-changing concept for the creative mind."
— **Morgan Swank, television writer/producer**

"This book doesn't just disrupt social media networking, it blows it up! You must read it, if you are a creative endeavoring in the field of music, film, tv, or the arts in general. Mark Maxwell, an entertainment attorney who doesn't bite, in fact he has a heart. A heart for God, the arts, and for young aspiring artists. His views on 'the ills' of networking and its impact on the creation of great art are evocative. Are we destined for a world that never produces another Michael Angelo or a Bob Dylan? Not if Mr. Maxwell has anything to say about it and he surely does."
— **L. Arthur Nichols, record producer**

"In the 26 years I have known Mark Maxwell as pastor and friend, he has always seen serving others as the very essence and expression of the mandate and ministry of Christ. This book captures beautifully this transformational truth. For Mark, the only true proof of real success is that the needs of others have been met and thus the divine purposes of God have been advanced. The principles of this book will work equally well in any context where people interact with one another. If the only real success is found through building real relationships that serve the real needs of others, *Networking Kills* provides a guidebook that will light and lead the way."
— **Dale Evrist, Senior Pastor, New Song Nashville**

"I truly enjoyed this! I share Mark's love of Bob Dylan so very much and his deep versatility has always been the most important inspiration and reference point for my own creative expression. I love Mark's sentiments and guidance about the modern condition of internet maintenance and entrepreneurship influencing artists...this is a daily struggle for me. I so appreciate how he weaves his spirituality into his professional practice."
— **Kim Logan, recording artist**

"Mark's book has really gotten to me. He absolutely has a gift, one of encouragement and hope that I really appreciate. I can't begin to tell you what a terrific blessing this book was for me. I must've taken 30 minutes to read certain paragraphs. His words really spoke to me at this time in my life. His life experiences and words have really reminded of God's promises for me and that I not be fearful of the unknown. Right now, I'm anticipating God's very best."
— **Roger Klein, entertainment executive & entrepreneur**

"Totally encouraged and challenged as I just read through Mark's book. I couldn't put it down, right through to the back cover. What a gracious and loving presentation of the relevance of Christ in your everyday! May many discover their purpose in Jesus; and other hearts be strengthened for the journey as mine has tonight!"
— **Dan Ingle, minister in South Asia**

"I really enjoyed this book. I actually had a few moments where I was a bit convicted about how I've treated some of the artist/writers that I have been working with over the past years. The fear that sometimes creeps up can change you from doing great work for everybody to 'what do they have to offer me' and it's easy to fall into the habit of working hard only for those who have the best chance to benefit me. I think I have some apologies in order. This is a very timely message that can benefit so many people."
— **Simon Gugala, record producer/songwriter**

MORE PRAISE FOR *NETWORKING KILLS: SUCCESS THROUGH SERVING* – FROM THE AUTHOR'S STUDENTS AND GRADUATES

"Everyone I know NEEDS this book. I've seen Mark live this so authentically in action with every life that he encounters and while it is a HUGE testament to the man of great respect and character that he is, it also flawlessly communicates the heart of God in such a profound way. One of my favorite quotes: 'I was trying to make myself visible, but God wants us to make ourselves available'—an easy trap so many young musicians and creatives can fall into trying to see their dreams realized. I needed to be encouraged, reminded and enlightened about so many things discussed here. It's so greatly impacted my life and needs to be taken to the world."
— **Alexa Cruse (27)**

"This book is filled with wisdom...I lost track of how many quotes I wrote down. Thankful for Mark's honesty, passion & skillful writing that left me hungry for more opportunities to serve and walk the road ahead with confidence. This book has had a profound impact on my train of thought, relationships with others, and my current assignments."
— **Taylor Agan (23)**

"This book could not have come at a better time. I have been applying to jobs for weeks here in LA, with no response to a single application I have sent in. I have been trying to build a community with what seems like slow progress and I've been contemplating quitting my job out of pure exhaustion and frustration. After reading Mark's book I realized I had not been aligning myself with God. I had been praying for responses to the applications I was sending in but never asked God to show me where He wanted me. I never gave him time to speak to me about His plan for my life. Mark's words caused me to stop in my tracks, take a different approach to the way I have been living and shift my focus to that of serving God and serving others."
— **Sela Rich (23)**

"I finished this book with a tear in my eye from the amazing story at the end. This book touches very real and deep questions in a perfectly story-crafted way that is easy and tangible to digest. Mark keeps the reader interested by using pop lyrics and relevant references in an amazing way! It is one of the best books I have ever read!"
— **Ian David Hodgdon (24)**

"This book wrecked me! It was absolutely what I needed to hear right now in so many ways. My favorite stories are Al Kooper, Johnny Cash, and honestly, anything personal to Mark and his family. This book is an absolute must for any students or aspiring entrepreneurs, but I also believe the concepts tackled are becoming increasingly relevant to people of all ages in today's fast-paced business world. Mark Maxwell brilliantly explains the inherent issues with modern day 'networking' and offers a practical approach to finding success and fulfillment through the act of serving. Highly recommend this read!"
— **Sean Fallon (26)**

"This book is a must read. My whole paradigm for my purpose in a professional industry and how to operate within it changed with this message—it cuts to the heart. So much wisdom in it about how to really live a full and joyful life. I was inspired at many points and even shed some tears while I was reading because I was that moved! Great stories, great lessons, great author!"
— **Alyssa Newton (21)**

"Professor Maxwell's class was always a highlight of my week. I have been questioning the direction my career should take and have been praying specifically for what I can do that will best serve God and others. Pursuing music often feels icky and fake at its worst and generally self-absorbed, even in the truest moments of creating. I'm tired of thinking about myself, my image, where money is going to come from. I don't know where I need to be going, but the encouragement and the affirmation I received from reading his stories of faith, reminds me that I am taken care of and planned for. I'm in a waiting period, learning to know God's voice when I hear it and praying for an assignment that I am certain of and that solves a problem in the world; and his book has given me such encouragement."
— **Katie Jones (25)**

"This book is so necessary for young creatives like myself! I've always hated the idea of networking (seems so self-serving and manipulative to me), but had simply accepted it as a necessary evil if I want to succeed. Mark's book changed that for me. The idea of living a life of service and creating friends rather than a life dominated by selfishness and creating contacts was a radical paradigm shift for me. I recently graduated from college and jumped into the creative industry, and have gotten the opportunity to put into action, and now have no fear that my success is reliant on how many peoples' hands I shake. Looking forward to using this method and rereading this book for the rest of my life."
— **Caleb Crino (22)**

"I loved it!! What an amazing approach to networking. Mark's real and transparent stories truly inspired me and served as a reminder to me that my purpose in my office and industry is to be a light."
— **Samantha Duffy (26)**

"I first met Mark Maxwell while I was still at my undergraduate (where Mark is a professor)--now I am heading into my final year of law school. The best part about Mark is that he truly does practice what he preaches, so to speak. Not only do I know this from personally witnessing it, this is evident throughout the text of his book. I completely agree with the main theory of the book; networking events have always left me feeling disingenuous, while having a service-oriented mentality has always bode me well. The few networking events I have gone to, feel very cheap and I feel like I am being completely selfish. Like without saying it, there is this unwritten acceptance of 'You know why I am here. Are you willing to help out a near total stranger?' I thought the book was really captivating. I loved the openness and vulnerability Mark showed throughout it. Overall, I thought it was a great read."
— **Riley Bauer (24)**

"My first steps into the music industry were happening while I was taking a course taught by Mark Maxwell, and the wisdom he imparted has affected every opportunity I've had. I can honestly say my success so far is directly related to the way he has guided myself and his other students to approach networking differently. My coworkers and bosses have all noticed and commented on the difference they notice between myself and other interns they've had—and it's because of this book. So honest, so helpful, so beautifully written. Amazing wisdom, incredible stories, and a true look at what the music industry needs. It will change your career, and for the much better."
— **Allie Gray (20)**

"*Networking Kills* is a timely message for this Millennial generation. The bill that has been sold to us by University leadership and professionals alike about networking and building your brand takes you into the mindset of working out of the need to grow a connection to only benefit you and your future career. Mark destroys that narrative with his counter intuitive approach to building relationships and serving others for the benefit of building someone else up rather than yourself. By being intentional about building real relationships with others, you can grow your business connections as well. This millennial generation is screaming for authenticity and this is exactly what Mark delivers."
— **Caleb Tannehill (24)**

"This book has opened my eyes to see art and professional life as a road to service and love instead of a way to lifestyle, popularity or money. I never thought of artists as servants to people or God, but this book showed me what that looks like. I think every young adult must read this book. The idea of serving has escaped my generation and left many to feel like they lack a purpose, including me. This book puts purpose in everything through a raw, beautiful testimony, and by rearranging the way a professional life is seen. While everyone else around me is telling me why networking gets you where you want to be, this book has shown me how service and obedience to God gets you where you need to be."
— **Samuel Soto (18)**

"As a young professional in the process of building a few small businesses, the idea of networking has always been icky to me, but I never actually realized there was a 'way out' until I read *Networking Kills*. I have been on both sides of the networking equation, trying to get something out of somebody and being the one approached to be used for something. I always believed there must be a better way than 'win/win' equations that are based in selfish ambition, but never really knew how to put it into words. Mark's book has encouraged me to step back and not depend on myself or clients or 'contacts,' but to live a life of service and trust God to be my provider."
— **Brandon Dragan (32)**

"From the beginning of a college student's education, the concept of 'networking' is drilled into their heads with the common saying, 'It's all about who you know.' I was one of those students, and early in my career I often left networking scenarios disheartened, with a bit of a slimy feeling having forced this 'networking' thing. Mark's book helps to put the aspiring business professional's ambitions of money, fame, and power into an eternal perspective. It makes you take a good look at what might seem like a secular career, and helps you see it through the lens of Jesus' teaching. We are all here on this earth to serve others whether pastors, rock stars, or business power players."
— **Danny Berrios (29)**

"What an honestly great read. It came at a perfect time in my life, I just couldn't put it down. I very much appreciate the honesty and wisdom put into it. As a young professional, I thought this book served as a solid reminder of how to truly network in any business environment. Mark was such a great professor to me at Belmont and his impact on my life is greater than I can express. This would make a great gift for any current college student too."
— **Claire Tallerico (27)**

"Mark's book is so important, regardless of what industry you work in (even though the focus is the entertainment industry) because students are told how important networking is from day one, as Mark says. It's so relieving to know that networking doesn't have to feel self-centered, and can feel fulfilling and rewarding when looking at networking the way Mark describes in his book. I've been fortunate enough to be able to put what Mark says into practice and can say that it works really well. Professional relationships are so much richer, and even the smallest tasks are fulfilling when putting Mark's words into action. As I start law school in a few weeks, I know I'll continue to look at networking through the lens Mark has described in his book."

— **Kendall Deranek (22)**

"Just, WOW. A MUST READ! This is not just a book, this is a world changing, God-given revelation that Mark has lived out, and the fruit speaks for itself. In a culture where platform seems to be created and maintained by 'shaking hands,' *Networking Kills* pierced my heart and opened my eyes to the truth: my hands aren't made for getting for myself, but rather, giving of myself. This book reminded me that we are born empty handed, and we will leave the same way. I pray *Networking Kills* spreads like wildfire among my generation because this book is a game changer, and a gateway message to a better world."

— **Rachel Hale (25)**

"I come away from reading this fantastic book of advice remembering that anything in this crazy music industry (or other industries) is a channel of God's provision for me, that I literally have nothing to fear because He alone will provide for me in this life and bring joy to my heart. Maxwell reminds us that no one, no matter how bruised and battered you are or have caused others to be, is out of God's reach, and you may just be the person He uses to reach someone like that."

— **Caylea Hering (22)**

"When making big decisions in the path of my life within the music industry, I often came to a fork in the road where one direction was a more visible and glamorous path and the other a considerably less glamorous path that would require more humility and behind-the-scenes work. Professor Maxwell's book speaks into these decisions, giving examples from his own life to illustrate the importance of weighing the world's often shallow definition of success against God's calling to serve."

— **Mikayla Foote (22)**

"*Networking Kills* is a must-have for anyone who wants to have a successful career in the music business. As a young man with a Christian upbringing stumbling along a career path that was carved by Hank Williams Sr., I constantly feel the dissonance between how the industry says I need to live my life and network versus the way Jesus teaches us to live and interact with others. Maxwell's book offers insight and real-world successful examples of how to live in a Christ-like manner while pursuing a career in the entertainment and music business. The key to success, just as the Lord instructs, is through service and 'loving your neighbor.'"

— **Tristen Smith (25)**

"I am lucky to have experienced the kindness and wisdom conveyed throughout this book firsthand. Mark Maxwell is a leader that came into my life at the exact right time and it is a gift to be able to hold so many of the lessons he has taught me in my hands through this book. In my experience, many are drawn to the music or entertainment industry through a love for the arts, then find themselves lost in the shuffle as purpose and intention become blurry. This book offers so many nuggets of wisdom and reassurance that working from love and passion will translate to success in your professional life. No matter your spiritual outlook, Maxwell proves the golden rule can apply anywhere: treat others as you want to be treated; what you put out into the world you will also receive. A must read!"

— **Elle Hussey (23)**

"Mark is my favorite professor and his book touched me. I truly enjoyed reading about his life and the ways in which he has served others. I love what he wrote about stage fright. That is something I have struggled with so much, but never stopped to think that it wasn't about me but about what I can give to others."

— **Abbie Nixon (20)**

"I just finished reading Professor Maxwell's book a couple days ago, and my goodness, it was incredible. There were numerous times while reading it that I literally had chills, because the content was extremely relevant and completely opened my eyes to an entirely different perspective. I wish every teen, every person in the music industry, every human being would read this book because I truly believe it can serve them in many ways. It has impacted the way I go about my job, my daily life, my relationships and my career, all through the grace of God and serving others through Him."

— **Anna Eisch (18)**

NETWORKING ~~S~~KILLS

SUCCESS
THROUGH
SERVING

MARK H. MAXWELL

DESOLATION ROW PRESS

NASHVILLE

To my children, students and clients:
the next generation of creatives,
business leaders and
world-changers I love.

TABLE OF CONTENTS

INTRODUCTION

The key to finding success in life and a meaningful career isn't about who you know, but how you serve. So many people say they want to make a difference and be successful along the way, but they ultimately get bogged down and veer off track by chasing inauthentic relationships, obsessively collecting social media "likes," and narcissistically building their "brand" and "story." There is a better way, and that way is approaching your life and career with the heart of a servant—putting other people first and building relationships with no strings attached.

To experience true success and fulfillment, and in an effort to obey God, this lens of serving must become the basis for all of our daily decision-making and our major life assignments. Serving attracts us to and is attractive to others when people can sense you genuinely care—then walls come down and true relationships form. And that is more powerful than any business card exchange, forced cocktail hour conversation or Instagram follow.

That is how you can truly make a difference in the world—one person at a time. In the pages ahead, you will learn how you can change the world by: *making yourself available instead of visible, giving instead of taking and losing yourself instead of finding yourself.*

MIXTAPE

A chapter-by-chapter companion mixtape
is available on Spotify as a playlist titled
"Networking Kills: Success Through Serving."

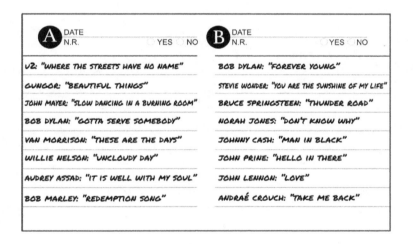

A DATE N.R.		YES NO		**B** DATE N.R.		YES NO
U2: "WHERE THE STREETS HAVE NO NAME"				BOB DYLAN: "FOREVER YOUNG"		
GUNGOR: "BEAUTIFUL THINGS"				STEVIE WONDER: "YOU ARE THE SUNSHINE OF MY LIFE"		
JOHN MAYER: "SLOW DANCING IN A BURNING ROOM"				BRUCE SPRINGSTEEN: "THUNDER ROAD"		
BOB DYLAN: "GOTTA SERVE SOMEBODY"				NORAH JONES: "DON'T KNOW WHY"		
VAN MORRISON: "THESE ARE THE DAYS"				JOHNNY CASH: "MAN IN BLACK"		
WILLIE NELSON: "UNCLOUDY DAY"				JOHN PRINE: "HELLO IN THERE"		
AUDREY ASSAD: "IT IS WELL WITH MY SOUL"				JOHN LENNON: "LOVE"		
BOB MARLEY: "REDEMPTION SONG"				ANDRAÉ CROUCH: "TAKE ME BACK"		

SCAN FOR PLAYLIST:

PART 1

BEING BORN

X

I was born very far from where I'm supposed to be,
and so I'm on my way home.
— Bob Dylan

CHAPTER 1
KIBERA

"Where the Streets Have No Name"
— U2[1]

The odor of the slum slapped us in the face like a forceful wave—it was unbearable. Nothing like anything I had experienced.

I struggled to keep walking ahead without throwing up. There were deceased animals and dogs that were walking dead. The pathways were sometimes split with trenches filled with sewage. We had to make running leaps over several.

Packs of young, shirtless men stared us down. I don't remember ever feeling so white, rich, American, obvious—and vulnerable. My eyes caught the eyes of a few of those young men. I wanted to glance into their souls to feel just a little of the pain they felt. My glances were not welcomed.

We struggled to keep up with our African guide, and a couple of times I feared he had lost us in the unmarked maze. My face flushed, my heart raced and my feet pounded swiftly ahead. Somehow, we found our guide again after making two quick rights and one left through the narrow alleyways and duck downs. As we walked, someone explained the "flying toilets": the burst baggies that littered every square of the red earth. The "flying toilet" has become the residents' answer to the lack of latrines or toilets. A flying toilet involves defecating into a plastic bag and throwing the bag into the street at night. I knew there was no way the tennis shoes I was wearing would be making the flight home with me to Nashville.

I had never truly witnessed poverty at this level before. It was complete sensory overload.

This was it. This *was* poverty.

Every single sight, turn, scent, home, mother, child, young person I saw broke my heart.

Broke it. Again. And again.

I knew poverty was real. But not this real.

This was hell.

✝ ✝ ✝

I really did not want to go.

It was not my fit and way outside my comfort zone.

The plane took off very, very late. *Of course!* There is nothing quite like attempting to lay horizontal in a narrow airplane seat, desperately trying to sleep, while others are busy reading their eyes out with those little beams of light at three a.m. They looked like over-zealous college students cramming information into their brains for finals! Go to sleep! Please! Of course, we missed our connecting flight in London. Next flight was eight hours later. *Okaaay.*

We finally arrived in Nairobi, Kenya, 30 hours after waving goodbye to Nashville. But our luggage did not! And it did not arrive the next day, or the next, or the next, or the next. Ultimately, instead of Africa, I suppose our clothes and personal items were more interested in seeing the world. They chose the "around-the-world tour" three, maybe four, consecutive times. So, during most of our time in Kenya, I had the privilege of wearing borrowed clothes and using someone else's toiletries. Awesome. I was able to hit the ground running on this continent with a fresh new style, image and scent. My first day in Nairobi was like waking up after taking the "red pill" to be shocked into finding I was now a cyberpunk rebel, groggily wandering about in a half-wake state in this new, unfamiliar dream-world— a *Matrix* of Africans, red dirt, unleashed animals and no traffic laws. Well, at least I had those little red bootie airline socks I could wear and call my own.

"What up with the red socks, *muzungu?*"

"Ugh, never mind."

But, we were there. We actually made it to Africa! I was really excited! I had my pocket bottles of hand gel and a nice stash of protein bars as back-up, just in case I was not sure what sort of meat was being served at a meal. Both came in *prett-y* handy on that trip. Secretly slipping into a bathroom to quickly gobble a protein bar worked fine. The only problem with hand sanitizer is that it is impossible to sneak a squirt under the table. That darn scent gave it away every time.

"Maxwell, what's that smell? Hand gel, again? C'mon!"

Just five weeks earlier, as I was stepping into my Sunday morning church service, John, our Missions Pastor, intercepted me and got all up in my face.

"I'm going to Nairobi next month, and I think you are supposed to go with me. I need your help serving our missionaries there."

Yeah, right, I thought. That is *not* happening. I have too many responsibilities in my law practice to travel on such short notice. My family needs me here. Besides, I don't want to go to Africa. I have thoroughly enjoyed supporting the work of our church missionaries in Africa as a friend and non-profit board member. I love the work Bono, my friends at Blood Water Mission, and others are doing there, but there is no reason I need to go there. I can do all I need to do to lead, financially support and pray for those ministries from right here in Nashville, TN. Now, don't get me wrong. My heart is there. I just don't want to actually *go* there.

Throughout the worship service, I squirmed.

God began to say: "Yep, he's right. You are going."

"No Lord. Please, no."

I had a lovely thought visualizing the Serengeti of the *Lion King,* but I knew I could watch Simba, Pumbaa and Timon anytime I wanted right here in my own living room at home.

"I have some work for you there that only you can do."

"No, God! There must be someone else who can go. You must have someone else who can help who would really love the idea of an Africa trip."

Throughout the service, my wife, Carol, kept looking over at me.

"What is wrong with you?"

"Nothing."

"Are you going to be okay?"

"I'm not sure."

As the service ended, I told Carol not to worry. I just needed to go spend some time with God and I would be home later.

I ended up parking in a Starbucks lot, and with teary eyes I continued my negotiation with God.

"Are you sure about this? Is this really necessary?" I asked him. "I am not qualified for this assignment. What will I even say? How can I help? What about my other responsibilities?"

Desperately, I pleaded: "*Please* send someone else, but not me!"

In hindsight, I realize how much my selfish excuses sounded like Moses arguing with God about his assignment to return to Egypt to face Pharaoh. Excuse after excuse.

Finally, I emotionally conceded. And as I did, I received peace and assurance from God that he would go with me. My heart's desire is to always obey God. I know there is true life when we yield ourselves to his plans. And I truly did want to serve our missionary family in Nairobi. I loved them dearly. They needed our help and leadership, and I wanted to see their sacrificial work with impoverished Kenyans flourish and multiply. I wanted to see more lives changed. Little did I know, God had an additional plan up his sleeve that would radically change *my* life, too.

The Kibera in Nairobi is the largest urban slum in Africa and the second largest slum in the world. At the time of my visit, it was estimated to contain over one million people crammed into its one-square-mile area. Seventy-five percent of the people living there are under 18, and 100,000 are orphaned. Life in the slum is dehumanizing and characterized by extreme poverty, corruption, rape, assault and contagious disease due to environmental pollution. There is little education or medical care, and HIV is rampant. Children and youth sit idle, often getting addicted to drugs and alcohol. The majority of the slum residents are reduced to begging to earn a living, and most earn less than $1.00 per day.

The typical Kibera home is a 12-x-12-foot shack built with mud and dung walls, a corrugated tin roof and mud floors. Many house eight or more family members, and they all sleep on the mud floor. Most shacks have no electricity, and clean water in Kibera is pretty scarce. There are no toilet facilities and their sewage runs downhill in open trenches which leads to insects and unimaginable odor. The rainy season in Kibera brings misery, disease and destruction as houses leak, collapse, and are washed away and pathways and roads become impassable due to flooding and refuse.

Our missionary family had built a sewing ministry for women living in Kibera. They sewed and laughed side-by-side with these women, making African clothing items that could be sold in the United States and other nations to meet the needs of their families. In addition to practical provision, these women were being nurtured, discipled and taught the Bible by our missionaries. One afternoon, we visited these women at a make-shift location on the outer edge of the slum. There were two dozen women present that day. Most had a number of children, and they were the sole providers for their family. A few had husbands, but otherwise the fathers of their children were either dead or gone. Every single one of these women was HIV positive and several had infants who were also infected.

In addition to their poverty, many of these women had faced sexual violence, abandonment and other illnesses, along with ongoing cultural discrimination due to HIV. It was a true honor to share a meal with this group of beautiful and brave ladies and to have an opportunity to share some smiles, a short Bible teaching and some prayer that day. They stole my heart.

After lunch, we were given the opportunity to hike into the depths of Kibera to visit one of the ladies' homes to see first-hand the daily life in the slum. We were supplied with a conscientious Kenyan guide for our safety and to help us find our way in and out of the maze of narrow, unmarked streets and pathways. We began our walk on a wide red-dirt road split by a railroad track, but soon our guide darted off into a maze of red dirt and muddied pathways lined with rows and rows of tiny homes. The stench was nauseating. It made your knees buckle. The quick, sloshing steps past inquisitive faces was heartbreaking. It was a death march.

Surrounded by these horrors, I was still struck by hope from something I noticed. We saw groups of very small children, some in brightly colored school uniforms, moving along in lines while holding hands, and playing together, laughing, jumping and smiling as if they had no care in the world. Somehow, they were oblivious to the pain, pressure and poverty that surrounded their lives. Their smiles and laughter were in sharp contrast to the blank, angry and broken expressions of the teens and adults we saw along the maze, whose lives and predicament had stolen their child-like hope and joy. But those little children were still marked with innocence, trust and faith.

Finally, we arrived at the sewing lady's home. Ducking under the doorway of this little shack in the middle of Kibera, we found ourselves in almost complete darkness. No electricity. A low ceiling. A mud floor. The shack was probably 10-x-10-feet: very tiny. There were few belongings on the floor or walls. This woman lived there with her five children. She politely welcomed us in.

I stood in the dark feeling paralyzed with grief because of the sights I had just witnessed getting to our destination and feeling the unfathomable weight of poverty as I stood looking around at the details of her "home." A little eight-year-old girl suddenly appeared in the shack. Our missionary friend explained that this little girl's only living relative died last week and this woman would now be taking her into her home and caring for her along with her other children.

"Mark, before we head back, would you be willing to pray over this little girl and for this household?"

"Of course."

Silence.

More silence.

I wanted to pray but nothing would come out.

I had no words.

I put my hand on top of the little girl's head and peeked through my closed eyes a little. My son back home in Nashville was also eight. I thought of him. His life in *my home*. I squinted down at her head, her clothes and her feet. No shoes! Her feet were bare! Here, I had already planned on burning or throwing my shoes away after one brief trip through the streets of Kibera and she *lives* here—*without shoes*.

I finally stammered out a prayer. We said our goodbyes. I never really could look that little girl square in the eyes. I honestly can't adequately describe all that I felt in those moments.

We burst out of the darkness of that shack into the blinding bright, hot sunshine and putrid smells of the streets. I wanted to get out of Kibera as fast as I could. I could not take the heartbreak and the pain. It was smothering. I remember jetting back out of that maze of pathways, stumbling through clothes lines of colorful African garments, down the red dirt paths, and past the dung-lined huts. Everything I had carefully noted and absorbed on the journey into Kibera was now a fast-motion, frenzied blur of escape that looked like those camera-shaking action scenes from a Jason Bourne movie. I was blinded by my tears, but fortunately, they were hidden by my Ray Bans.

Two weeks after I returned from Kenya, I was upstairs in my home working out. Life was somewhat back to normal. In the middle of that workout, I began to worry about our finances. We had some unexpected tax issues that were going to be costly. My worry and stress began to escalate.

In the middle of those thoughts, God suddenly transported me back to that little 10-x-10-foot hut, back to the sewing woman who would now be caring for six children, not five, back to that little eight-year-old girl with no shoes. God began to replay the HD video of that Kibera moment in my head while I stood on the second floor overlooking 4,500 square feet of my American home. I was worried? I was scared about my finances? How utterly outrageous. *I am disgusting.*

I fell flat on my face on the floor and cried. No, I sobbed. I cried louder and longer and harder than I have ever cried in my life. In those moments I asked God to please forgive me for not trusting him to provide for me and my family. He had promised that so clearly in so many ways, and I was wrong not to fully trust him and believe him. His promise to me to provide was burned and tattooed into my heart that day.

But what about that orphan girl I prayed for in the hut? What do I do about that? What do I do about her? In those moments of tears on the carpet, God supernaturally ripped out my "old" heart and gave me a "new" heart for the poor, for the orphan, for the fatherless. I had always known and understood the needs out there were great. I had prayed, gone on mission trips, and I had given resources to those needs. But that day, those needs went from my mind, from my head, to my heart. I believe that day God generously gave me his heart for the poor, the orphan and the fatherless. It was unreal. No, actually it was very real and tangible. I was reborn that day. I was changed.[2]

Over the next eighteen months, God did some powerful things in me. There were spiritual changes in me that manifested physically. I began to lose weight— unintentionally. That year I lost 35 pounds. I would awake each day with this deep, hollow empty feeling along with an accompanying high. It was similar to fasting for 24 hours, or sort of like that moment at the top of the roller coaster where your stomach drops out as you begin the steep descent. In my journal entry dated April 18, 2009, I wrote: "*Back here from Nairobi 5 weeks. Still have 'hollow-butterfly' feeling. I don't fully understand. Still need to embrace more of what You have for me. I feel like I am on the edge of a cliff. And You are saying, 'Jump! I've got you. Come Away with Me.'*"

This deep hollowness lasted most of each day and every day for well over a year. Ask any of my friends. They will recall our conversations and prayers about those mind-boggling days. God was burning out old worldly things in my inner self while making me into a new carrier of his life; a new wineskin was required for new wine, to use the analogy Christ describes in the Gospel of Matthew.[3]

I sensed God had set all of this in motion to bring about some big changes in our lives, our focus and in my career.

Maybe I was supposed to completely give up my entertainment law practice. Maybe we were supposed to move to Africa to serve in some way. Maybe I could shift my legal work into an organization like World Vision, Compassion International, or International Justice Mission, where I could begin to make a difference in the lives of orphans and the fatherless. I wanted to figure out how to help protect the smiles and laughter of young children like the ones I saw in Kibera and to help restore the smiles and laughter to those older ones who had been abandoned or broken. I began to make phone calls to friends I knew in those organizations. *What do you think? Could there be an assignment for me like that?* Carol and I began to pray, asking for God's next assignment for us.

Simultaneously, God began to give me a new sensitivity and love toward young people, especially those who had been orphaned or who had been abandoned or neglected in any way by their father. In fact, God began to bring dozens of young people into my and Carol's and my children's lives who fit that description. Without searching for them, they found us, and he began to give us favor and relationship and grace to begin to serve their needs.

It all started with Carol's precious niece Melody who moved from Newport Beach to come live with our family that year. She changed our family's life in a revolutionary way. She moved in with us as Carol's niece, then after a year, she moved back to

California as my niece. Then, a few more came to live in our home, some amazing ones came into our lives through our church home group, some through our Monday night dinner gatherings, some came in through our youth group, and some through a new church plant we initiated.

It was really something. It was like God helped the Maxwells to magically remove the doors to our hearts and home and all of these young people began to flood in. And the more we opened up our hearts and home, the more they came. It was not that we had necessarily been closed off before; Carol and I have always valued mentoring young students, engaged couples and others. I suppose we had subtly held certain things back in terms of our time and resources. During these new days, God was teaching us to lay all of our time and resources before him and ask God: "Ok, who gets these today?"

Six months after Kibera, I walked out the front door of Bongo Java coffee house, directly across the street from Nashville's Belmont University (Bongo is Nashville's first legit coffee house. Carol and I were at their grand opening weekend all the way back in 1993 when we first moved to Nashville from Los Angeles). I had just finished a late-night Bible study upstairs with some young people. Little did I know at the time, God was just about to answer my post-Kibera prayers about a new career and ministry assignment. As I stood alone on the

Bongo Java outdoor deck, everything was quiet and peaceful. I looked over at Belmont University and God said:

"You are supposed to be on that campus."

He was very clear. That moment was profound. But I thought, "Doing what?"

A few weeks later, a dear music industry friend introduced me to the Dean of the Belmont University Music Business School, a thriving and world-recognized program. The meeting was short, but warm. I really did not know what to say to the Dean. I did not think that starting with, "God told me I was supposed to be on this campus," would get me very far with him.

So, I told him about my history in the music business, and I mentioned that, years earlier, I had spoken at a seminar and judged a student talent competition on campus. Maybe I could do that again. He nodded. I said perhaps I could meet and counsel with graduating seniors who are considering law school. He nodded.

Then he said, "Or, perhaps you could be an Adjunct Professor for us."

"Yes, maybe I could be an Adjunct Professor. Wait, what's an *Adjunct Professor?*"

CHAPTER 2
WATCH YOUR STEP

Every place that the sole of your foot will tread upon
I have given to you... [1]

"Beautiful Things"
— Gungor[2]

The thump and whistle of The Black Keys *Brothers* album and the haunting strings and space in that great *Gungor* record had been our soundtrack that summer of 2010. My 10-year-old son, Harrison, and I had blood-bonded on a cross-country road trip where he and I experienced half of the U.S. while my wife, Carol, and my 13-year-old daughter, Sophia, traveled on a mission trip to Mexico. "H-man" and I both lived to tell about our teeth-baring facedown of the one hundred and twenty miles per hour Top Thrill Dragster roller coaster at Cedar Point (praying out loud for the entire 30-second ride was the key for me). For July 4th, he and I joined almost a million fellow patriots by squeezing onto the hallowed stone steps of the Lincoln Memorial (right near MLK's and Bob Dylan's historic spot in 1963!). We shared tears and lumps in throats as our eyes and skin reflected the magnificent explosions of the fireworks. It was powerful!

H and I traveled light that summer. I slapped together our peanut butter and honey combo on thin wheat bread in the bright sun on our SUV tailgate a couple of times a day. Harrison put away Twizzlers and Monster drinks like a champ.

Most days, his only complaint was: "Dad, my thumb STILL hurts!"

"H, look in that glove box and pop another Advil. You'll be fine!"

When we returned in victory to Nashville after our two weeks together on the road, Carol (Harrison's responsible parent) took him to the doc just to make certain the young warrior's thumb was okay. Surprise! It had been fractured since the opening night of our father-son adventure.

Then summer ended.

Standing before a table of cool college students in the Belmont University cafeteria, I was fairly confident. Packed and ready, but not exactly clear where this journey would lead. Or how it was going to change my life. Just one month earlier, Harrison and I had been touring the United States Capitol when I received the call from Belmont requesting I teach a class that fall.

At the window table at the back of the cafeteria, I had spied a young blonde singer with attitude named Gabrielle.

I had watched her grow up in our church. I headed that way past the aroma of college gourmet delicacies (wink). This moment at Belmont seemed like miles from those church memories, but I hoped our old connection might smooth my transition from the "real world" to the "college world" that night.

"Hey Gabrielle! Hey guys, how are you?" She introduced me to her artsy friends around the table. One was Marshall. He was 6' 6" (at least), lean, soft spoken, with Warby Parker glasses. He moved around town on a vintage bicycle and was an entrepreneurial leather craftsman. Down the table was Adrienne, a confident and striking actress and fellow Texan with an imaginative tomboyish haircut. Her look was a cross between Audrey Hepburn and David Bowie. Marshall and Adrienne would eventually become students of mine and close friends of my family.

I was not invited to sit down, which was fine.

I started off: "You know, this is my first night teaching. I am very excited. My class meets every Thursday night from 6:30 to 9:15. Kinda long."

"Awesome!"

"Wow!"

"What class?"

"Survey of the Music Business."

"You are going to do great!"

"One question for you guys. I was thinking about starting off my class each night with prayer. Am I allowed to do that as a professor?"

Their responses were all over the map.

"Interesting…I have never had a professor do that since I've been at school here."

"Wow, not sure. Some students might get a little offended by that."

"If it's something you really want to do, you should just do it!"

"I am not sure you are allowed to do that…"

Adrienne said, "Hey, this is a private school, so you can definitely do it. I think that would be great."

That settled it.

Just a few minutes before that cafeteria meeting, I had crossed that not-so-invisible threshold into "college world" when I felt the soles of my feet step onto the Belmont University campus that late August evening. Goosebumps. This was a new life assignment from God that I could not have predicted.

My walk continued.

I strode into my classroom and stood eye-to-eye and heart-to-heart with thirty 18-year-olds from all over the country who sat below that weird clock on the back wall that referenced Honolulu time. I had begun studying their names, hometowns, and degree plans a month earlier. These young ones had just left high school, Mom and Dad, family and friends to pursue their childhood dreams of life, music, songwriting and the music and entertainment business in Nashville. And those dreams were parked in the desks at the feet of "Professor Maxwell." This was not just my threshold, it was theirs. This was big. This was serious.

Suddenly, the weight of the stewardship of these fragile young hearts began to feel heavy. Fear struck hard. All confidence evaporated.

What am I doing here? Why me? I am not qualified for this responsibility. How am I going to lecture for three hours? What was I thinking? What can I give them of value? I'm a fool. Oh God! Wait, I must pray. That was it. Wait, what should I pray? I never thought about what I would pray. Lord, maybe I should pray that I don't screw these kids up! Pray that I don't disappoint them. What if I don't make sense? What if they laugh at me?

Wait...it's not about me. It's about THEM.

I am here to serve them. That is my role.

That is my assignment. God's assignment for me. To love. To give. To serve. THEM.

I will pray for THEM. That is how I will begin each night of class.

"I am honored to meet you all tonight, and I am so excited to have the opportunity to serve each one of you this semester. Welcome to Belmont! Welcome to Nashville! Before we get started tonight, I would like to take a moment to pray for all of you. Would you close your eyes and join me?"

"Father, thank you for my students. I pray that you would bless each one of them with wisdom, health, joy, laughter, creativity, inspiration, encouragement, real friendships, etc., etc. In Jesus name, Amen."

My eyes opened. Their eyes opened.

Supernatural peace and confidence.

Deep love and purpose.

"OK class, let's get started…"

Over the course of my thirty-year career as a record company executive and entertainment attorney, in my counsel to young performing artists, I frequently assure them that the key to overcoming stage fright or the fear of bombing at a live show is to understand that when you stand on a stage, you have the honor of presenting your audience with a gift. You are there to love and serve your audience, not simply to receive their adoration and affirmation. Your voice, musicianship, melody and lyrics make up a beautiful, supernatural, creative gift, and you are vulnerably serving your audience by offering them joy, hope, perspective, empathy and love—a gift to transform their hearts and lives that night and beyond. It's always about the audience and not about you as the artist. Once an artist understands the power of that gift and makes that his or her primary focus instead of finding his or her identity in the applause, then the spotlight becomes a place of love instead of a place of fear with the risk of failure. On my first night as a professor at Belmont (and every night following), the counsel I had given to so many artists over the years became the lesson I needed, too. The professor became the student.

SERVING ERASES FEAR OF FAILURE

When your work is focused on others,
the fear of failure is gone.

PART 2

DEFINING SUCCESS AND NETWORKING

If I hear the word 'networking' one more time I'm gonna explode. Is that what life has come down to, finding people you can use to get ahead?
— Bob Lefsetz[1]

CHAPTER 3
WHY NETWORKING IS %@&#

Out, damned spot! Out, I command you!…
But who would have thought the old man would have
had so much blood in him?
— Lady Macbeth (incoherently rubbing imaginary blood from
her hands) *Macbeth*, Act 5, Scene 1

"Slow Dancing in a Burning Room"
— John Mayer[1]

Let me ask you a question I ask my students:

How would you define success or greatness for yourself in life? In other words, what do you want from life? What will it take for you to feel you have attained a well-lived life?

Think about this for a moment.

<u>Your Possible Answers:</u>
A loving family.
True and loyal friendships with others.
A strong marriage.
To be known.

To be loved.

Living life to the fullest.

A self-sustaining business.

Confidence and purpose in who I am.

Community respect.

Joy and happiness.

To be a respected leader.

To be a visionary.

To be a fearless innovator.

Fame.

A meaningful career.

Showing justice and mercy to others.

Financial independence.

A healthy life.

Intimacy with God.

Leaving a legacy.

Making the world a better place.

What are your definitions of success or greatness for yourself in life that are not included on this list?

Merriam Webster defines success as "the fact of getting or achieving wealth, respect or fame." Today, the voice of the culture, media and education is proclaiming ever louder that the path to success or greatness for yourself in life must be achieved through networking. So, what is the definition of networking?

Networking is defined as the cultivation of relationships that can help you advance or move to a higher position.

The current order of the day is that any valuable achievement in life which involves relationships, whether in business, marriage, social justice or entertainment, *must* be fueled by the self-serving methods of networking.

Freshman college students are pummeled with this mantra by career counselors for four long years up through and following graduation in their job search efforts. You must show up, meet others and make yourself known. Young professionals, creatives and entrepreneurs are often convinced networking is the only way to build clients, new businesses, and business relationships, and there is no other choice in the matter. You must build relationships with others whether or not you really know or care about them. That is the key to your future. Singles hop to bigger events, larger churches and grander social events in order to increase their pool of eligible spouses. That is just the way it is in life these days.

A few weeks ago, a well-known artist manager described a young successful music executive to me this way: "I know Joshua. He is amazing. He networks at the highest level."

Become a master networker, and the world is yours.

Whether you are a young hip hop artist trying to get your music heard and out there, or you are an entrepreneur with a creative new business idea looking for backers, or a college senior desperately searching for your first "real" job, networking—just like death and taxes—appears to be one more sad certainty in our lives.

+ + +

Celebrities, and all of us commoners as well, consciously and unconsciously validate their success and greatness through social media by the number of friends, followers, likes, and views they receive, whether or not those relationships are real or authentic. With the possibility of amazing financial rewards through advertising, opportunity and fame through social media networking today, in our drive to matter and succeed, we naturally begin to extend to other areas of our business and social lives the collection of large numbers of inauthentic relationships. Plus, for those of us who work in creative and technology arenas, there is a double-edged sword to social media networking.

A recent *Atlantic Magazine* article entitled, "The Death of the Artist and the Birth of the Creative Entrepreneur," claimed that success as a young creative is no longer about technique or expertise. Instead of the 10,000 hours of experience it takes to birth genius that Malcolm Gladwell espoused in his book *Outliers*, it is now about having 10,000 contacts, a customer-focused approach to art instead of one built on innovation, craft and beauty.[2] Gladwell proposes that superior creative genius is not about lightning striking or extraordinary God-given talents, but it more often percolates and blossoms through extended periods of intense and deliberate creative work and collaboration. In other words, John, Paul, George and Ringo would have never become the Beatles without the 10,000 hours they spent over several years banging out all-night live performances in the smelly, underground clubs of Liverpool and Hamburg. The prodigy story always makes a beautiful novel or movie—we all love it—but in most cases, it is a myth.[3]

Networking has become a deceptive and broken substitute for time-honoring, often isolated, passionate work in developing craft and expertise. Young creatives can now be prematurely lulled into a false sense of creative identity and success by the number of likes and followers on their social media networks. In 2010, pop artist John Mayer suddenly closed his Twitter social media account and confessed on his blog his own creative downfalls experienced from networking: "You can't create lasting art if you are heavily involved in social media. It occurred to me that since the invocation of Twitter, nobody who has participated in it has created any lasting art. And yes! Yours truly is included in that roundup as well. Those who decide to remain offline will make better work than those online. Why? Because great ideas have to gather. They have to pass the test of withstanding thirteen different moods, four different months and sixty different edits. Anything less is day trading. You can either get a bunch of mentions now or *change someone's life* next year[4] (italics mine)."

I wholeheartedly believe changing lives should be the goal of every great technological or artistic endeavor. Joe Strummer of The Clash stood proudly behind our societal need for "three chords and the truth." Steve Jobs asked Pepsi's John Sculley the question: "Do you want to spend the rest of your life selling sugared water or do you want a chance to change the world?" Music pundit, Bob Lefsetz, recently challenged the music community to wake up from its self-focused online stupor and write new protest songs of value that transform culture, like those from decades past: "We need middle class leaders speaking up compassionately for the disadvantaged. Don't worry about offending. Just by speaking your truth you're gonna @#$% off somebody. Don't let that hold you back. Great art has historically made people uncomfortable. You're doing it for society, not for yourself. Narcissism is passé. You're providing a service."[5] Bono's words remind us: "Music can change the world because it can change people."

Networking has also become a distraction and an inhibitor in the creative development process. Becoming a creative who can generate works with lasting cultural impact requires what Georgetown professor Cal Newport calls "deep work," which is a combination of working for extended periods of time with full concentration on a single task, free from distraction or interruption, followed by intermittent rounds of feedback. A process where one wrings every last drop of value out of his current intellectual capacities. Newport asserts that our creative abilities are improved by the mental strain that accompanies this "deep work."[6] Conversely, in a 2011 seminar with a group of our nation's top music students at Berklee College of Music, John Mayer explained how social media distraction actually narrowed his creative capacity: "The tweets are getting shorter, but the songs are still four minutes long. You're coming up with 140-character zingers, and the song is still four minutes long...I realized about a year ago that I couldn't have a complete thought anymore, and I was a tweetaholic. I had four million Twitter followers, and I was always writing on it. And I stopped using Twitter as an outlet and I started using Twitter as an instrument to riff on, and it started to make my mind smaller and smaller and smaller. And I couldn't write a song."[7]

Sadly, I am afraid our cultural addiction to social media networking is killing songs and artists before we ever get to hear their voices, melodies and ideas.

The year 2006 was the year Twitter was born and Facebook expanded outside the limited college market. That was also the same year John Mayer created his most beloved and acclaimed album recording, *Continuum*. Mayer took an extended break from Twitter from September 2010 to January 2014, just a little over three years. Will he ever be able to recapture the sort of musical magic found on *Continuum* again? As fans, we can only hope so. But, with the creativity displacement and distraction of social media networking nipping at John's heels, we may never get to hear it.

With the explosion of social media in the past 10 years, is it becoming more and more unlikely for creative geniuses and their groundbreaking works to develop and emerge? Could we be blindly standing in a new world where we will never again see mind-shattering songwriters and musicians crafting and communicating with the extraordinary brilliance of the Beatles, Miles Davis, Bob Dylan, and Stevie Wonder; or impassioned novelists whose life work transports us into stunning new worlds of imagination, like J.R.R. Tolkien and J.K. Rowling; or inspired painters who turn our world upside-down and produce beauty unseen before, like Van Gogh and Picasso; or fiery young filmmakers with the vision and capacity to capture the human condition and transform our souls with originality, like Steven Spielberg, Christopher Nolan and the Coen Brothers? Will we ever see another George Lucas or Jeff Bezos or Steve Jobs?

As a lover of great art, music, technology, and entertainment, that is a sad and scary assessment that is personally unbearable. Could we be moving toward the graveside of world-changing art and creative ingenuity? In the apocalyptic voice of music critic

Lester Bangs to William Miller in the film *Almost Famous* (citing the death of rock and roll): "It's over, you got here just in time for the death rattle."

✝ ✝ ✝

Networking is a force. It's big business. Trendy podcasts are packed with tempting networking ideas and approaches from shrill (and profane) voices who have discovered "the keys" we need: keys to wealth and happiness. The life success strategy of networking is rooted in the teachings of Dale Carnegie's classic book, *How to Win Friends and Influence People* and continues through modern-day *New York Times* business best-sellers by Tim Ferriss, Keith Ferrazzi, Harvey Mackay, Jordan Harbinger, and others. The business networking social media website LinkedIn was purchased in 2016 by Microsoft for $26.2 billion and has over 450 million members. A quick word search of the term *networking* on that site yields over 10 million hits under *people* and 160,000 hits under *work experience*, again illuminating the power and pervasiveness of the networking philosophy.

As a college professor and entertainment attorney, I spend a great deal of time meeting with college students, young business people and creatives. As I do, I hear a common reply to the mandatory networking message:

"I hate it, I don't want to do it, but I guess I have to do it in order to *make* it."

Typical responses to this success requirement range from those who are fearful and socially intimidated by such tactics all the way to those who are morally disgusted and emotionally sickened by the practice of networking strategies.

Many who attempt to network relay stories of uncomfortable rejection and insecurity. And those who are on the receiving end of networking often feel angry and offended by the silly phoniness, pushiness and insensitivity of the networker. I've been THAT guy. It's poisonous!

The problem with networking is that no matter how you slice it or dress it up (win/win, generosity to others, palms down, etc.), the root or foundation of networking is based on exploitation and selfishness, on taking from others and using others for your own benefit. And there is something deep inside of all of us (I will call it the image of God), that fights against that selfish pathway to success.

Networking contradicts the nature of our Creator that is found in us. His identity is centered on love—giving generously and sacrificially—not on taking and using.

But, networking is not just a spiritual problem; it also presents a psychological problem. A recent psychology study led by a Harvard professor reveals that participating in professional networking events creates feelings of physical dirtiness in those attending. Psychology research has shown that people think about morality in terms of cleanliness.

In other words, people feel physically dirtier (or morally impure) upon the reflection of past transgressions as opposed to recalling good deeds. Psychologists refer to these sorts of feelings as the "Macbeth Effect," referencing the Shakespearean scene in which a guilt-racked Lady Macbeth tries to wash imaginary blood off her hands. The Roman Pontius Pilate comes to mind for me as well.[8][9][10]

The results of this recent study showed that intentional professional networking increases feelings of inauthenticity and immorality, and therefore feelings of dirtiness, much more so than networking to just make friends or spontaneous networking that happens without prior self-centered motivation or planning.

If networking to achieve success actually makes you feel dirty or morally impure, how does the person being networked actually feel? In addition to feeling dirty, I would personally add words like violated and assaulted to describe the feelings of the network-ee.

NETWORKING KILLS *Creativity*

NETWORKING KILLS *Authentic Relationships*

NETWORKING KILLS *Life*

NETWORKING KILLS *Love*

Is there an alternative approach to success that avoids this moral dilemma?

A different approach that stops this crime?

How do we start and develop our careers and still keep our hands clean?

What is the answer?

Obviously, we all need others to share our lives with and partner with in order to experience fruitfulness, success and greatness in our communities, businesses and creative endeavors.

Together we *are* better.

Two *are* better than one.[11]

We really do need each other to change ourselves and to change the world. So, there MUST be a different and better path to success and greatness, *right?*

PART 3

THE SUCCESS OF CHRIST

Anybody can be great, because anybody can serve.
— Martin Luther King, Jr.

CHAPTER 4:
IT'S NOT ABOUT YOU

A life not lived for others, is not a life.
— Mother Teresa

*Don't live for yourself. That is too easy. You will gain
nothing from that endeavor. Live for others...
That is where you will find true riches in life.*
— Scooter Braun (manager for Justin Bieber,
Ariana Grande, Kanye West & Tori Kelly)

"Gotta Serve Somebody"
— Bob Dylan[1]

As an entertainment attorney, I represent a wide variety
of amazing creatives: young recording artists, songwriters and
producers, filmmakers and authors, as well as entertainment
companies of all kinds. I am a transactional attorney, which
means I handle entertainment contracts—no litigation or
appearances in court for me. I draft, review, negotiate and
provide counsel to creatives and creative companies concerning
recording artist agreements, music publishing agreements,

licensing agreements, producer agreements, management agreements and so on. I have clients who earn more money in one year than I will make in my lifetime, and I have others just getting their careers off the ground who can only compensate me in terms of Americanos and green tea. I thrive on that extreme variety of relationships, and I try to provide great service and value no matter what each client can afford to pay me. I love serving my clients. I am a counselor and connector of creatives. I view myself as a steward of their dreams, creativity and cultural influence. And I am honored to call so many of them close friends.

But, there is one group of potential clients that I have made it a personal principle to always turn down. I have never represented any minors, clients under the age of 18. With so many young teenagers becoming mega-star millionaires in the music business, I know my peers are perplexed by my view on this issue.

Here is why I take that stand. Number one, every state in the country says a minor may not legally sign a contract because he or she is simply too young for that kind of responsibility. And honestly, that is good enough for me. Now, there are some legal end-arounds. One is the possibility of taking that child before a judge to remove his or her minority status so a contract can still be legally signed. The second one is to attempt to shift the financial risk onto the minor's parents in the event that child tries to run from a contractual obligation.

But, for me, the biggest reason I turn away minors is the likelihood of family breakdown when children enter entertainment contracts while their parents are standing beside or behind them. These breakdowns often occur when the young artist is successful, but they also happen when they fail. I have witnessed the historical results, including divorce, bankruptcy, lawsuits, emotional trauma and severed relationships between spouses and between children and one or both parents. As a servant and steward, I will not risk one day standing before God and having to answer for those life-altering outcomes.

For the sake of success, many companies are happy to maneuver through all the risks and internal family "strings" with that underage artist; and, in the long run "Mom" or "Dad" often remains attached to that artist long after the child turns 18.

Oftentimes, those company decisions raise the specter of the pushy, networking, helicopter parent who is living out his or her own dreams of stardom through the entitled teenager or young adult, a scenario where so many entertainment executives are hopelessly drowning or are still experiencing haunted nightmares.

This is not new.

In the Bible, Jesus Christ got a first-hand taste of the modern entertainment executive's dilemma when Salome, the networking "stage mom," and her two wannabe sons, James and John, got up in Christ's face about the future fame, success and greatness of her two boys. Now, James and John were loved by Christ and were part of his inner circle. They were sold out and passionate, but they were also hard-boiled and contentious. Christ nicknamed these two Type A characters the "thunder sons." In unison, Mama S., with her sons at her side, asked Christ to award the brothers the highest place of honor in his Kingdom, one at Christ's right hand and one at his left hand. Fame. Authority. THE Two Greatest Positions. Nothing subtle about her request.

All of Christ's other close friends were ticked! A perfect example of networking fallout.

I will get to their actual conversation momentarily, but first off, think about Jesus, the One who is being networked in this little pow-wow. In order to understand the true definition of success and greatness and the pathway to their achievement, I think it is important to reflect on the wisdom of the smartest person who ever lived: Jesus Christ. Often, we are guilty of limiting our view of Christ to his other attributes, like him being the most loving, or the most merciful, or the most humble man who ever lived; but, we must also acknowledge that he was the smartest man who ever lived, too. He was a man of faith AND intellect.

Throughout his life, Jesus' striking intellectual abilities can be seen in his powerful stories and beautiful parables, his rigorous use of logic, his successful debates with rivals, his interpretations of the law, his reasoning from evidence, and his profound teachings and theological lessons.[2] Paul recognizes the preeminent intelligence of Christ by stating that he is the One "in whom are hidden all the treasures of wisdom and knowledge."[3] Theologian Dallas Willard challenges us to "understand that Jesus is a *thinker*, that this is not a *dirty word* but an *essential work*, and that his other attributes do not preclude thought, but only insure that he is certainly the greatest thinker of the human race: 'the most intelligent person who ever lived on earth.'"[4]

Because Christ, the Great Teacher, really loved this thunderous family, he embraced this uncomfortable confrontation, seeing it as an opportunity to redefine success and to instruct all of us about the true path to greatness. Salome came up to Jesus with her two sons to ask a favor. This mom makes Kris Jenner look like a beginner.

She demanded, "Jesus, fix it, so that my two sons will be awarded the highest places of honor in your kingdom—one on your right and one on your left."

He was taken aback and said, "You don't know what you are asking."

He looked deep into the eyes of her two future rock star sons: "If you want to be great, you must become a servant. If you want to be first, you must become like a slave. That's what I have done. I came to serve, not be served."[5]

So, he taught us that serving is not only the path to success, *it is SUCCESS.*

Serving is a pathway to success that is the opposite of the heart and motivation of networking. At its core, networking methodology is rooted in selfishness, taking and using, while Christ teaches us that *true* success comes through serving, giving generously, and loving others without reservation. It's important to recognize and understand that God's order and the culture's system of order are often polar opposites.

Jesus had the revolutionary habit of taking the things we have always believed or understood and completely redefining them. He took the cultural norms and standards of the existing world order and flipped them upside-down. Christ and the Bible do not only recommend serving in order to achieve success, serving others is actually a commandment. And not just any commandment; it is the essence or summation of all of God's laws in six words. In Galatians 5:14, St. Paul says: "For everything we know of God's word and His law is summed up in a single sentence: *Love others as you love yourself.*"

Jesus said if you want to be first, you must serve like a slave. Serving like a slave means your will is consumed with fulfilling the needs of another. Author John Bevere encourages us to reflect on the legacy of our greatest leaders. The leaders who inspire us. The ones we remember, quote and emulate long after they are gone. "Think about leaders like Martin Luther King, Jr. and Mother Teresa," he suggests. "They were consumed with serving the needs of those they loved. What about Stalin or Hitler? They were consumed with asserting their power over people. Executing their will upon people."[6]

To experience success and in an effort to obey God, this lens of serving must become the basis for all of our daily decision-making and our major life assignments.

A few months ago, I was mentoring a young music business executive in my law office. He was very excited about an affirming job offer he had received from another competitor company. He and his wife were committed to prayer for God's guidance in his decision, and they were seeking counsel from other leaders in their lives about this potential transition.

As we talked, he summarized what he was beginning to sense as God's next life assignment for him this way: "I believe that this new job and company will be great a place for me to grow."

"That is fine and very encouraging," I said. "But, I believe the primary question to ask first is whether this new job and company will be a great place for you to *serve others*. Will it be the *best* place for you to serve others *right now?* And, very importantly, do you sense the serving assignment at your current company is coming to a close?"

If you believe the teachings of Christ, every decision you make in life should be evaluated by your ability and God's current assignment to meet the needs of and to love and care for others. Our desire to grow, mature and gain experience in our careers and businesses must always come in second place to the care and serving of others.

Always.

It's not about you. It is *always* about others.

✠ ✠ ✠

When my son Harrison turned 16, that new doorway of manhood and freedom was marked by the passing of his driver's test. At his birthday party, Carol and I surprised him with the key to my old boxy Range Rover that we affectionately call The Beast. The Beast is black, born in 1989, and you will hear it coming before it arrives. The Beast will not stop running, although its air conditioning gave out years ago. H-man immediately began plotting all the improvements he had in mind for The Beast. First up was the addition of multi-colored floorboard lights that change color with the beat of the music. If you have ever seen the Richard Gere/Julia Roberts late 80's, LA-based chick flick Pretty Woman, you can catch a glimpse of what The Beast looked like in its youth. But, I guarantee Richard Gere did not have Harrison's sick floorboard lights.

With all of Harrison's newfound freedom, there were other exciting changes. Of course, The Beast only gets about 11 MPG and there will be other repairs down the road. So he and I began discussing various summer job ideas:

"Chick-fil-A?"

"Boring."

"How about that new Publix?"

"That would be really boring."

"How about the Juice Bar?"

"Nah, kind of boring."

Finally, I stopped him. "OK, enough with the 'boring!' I want to help you get a fresh vision for your first job. You must see this first job, and every job, as a place to serve others, not as a place for you to get your emotional needs met. Ask the question, 'Where is a place that is filled with people who need me and need my gifts?' Then step into that place desiring to bring life and joy to customers and co-workers. That's when you will have true purpose that enables you to get through the tough days at any job."

It's important to remember: *There is no dream job, but serving can create purpose and contentment that can make the most difficult (or boring) job feel like a dream.*

Oh, by the way, he nailed a job at Starbucks!

SERVING CREATES PURPOSE

When your work is centered on others,
purpose and contentment are found.

You see, no matter how young you are or how broken or unqualified you might feel, with serving, you can begin to see the love and care you share through your imperfect life radically changing the lives of others. Again, this is another example of how God flips the world order with *his* order of things.

How does this work? A young Florida pastor named Rich Wilkerson, Jr. says, "Your wounds can become someone else's wisdom. Your pain can become someone's else's medicine. Your breakdown can become someone else's breakthrough. Why? Because I'm not here for me, I'm here for everyone else around me."[7]

Networking repels and divides, while serving attracts and is attractive. As your heart for serving grows, you are attracted to people and situations you would have previously avoided or never noticed. And when someone feels loved and cared for by you through your serving, his barriers and fears come down. When a patient, enduring love is received by another, he wants more of it and wants to share it with others. It's beautiful! When someone experiences something beautiful, he desperately wants to show it to others. A natural multiplication of love and relationship follows.

We all dream of being people who can truly change the world. Who leave a mark. Sometimes our dreams and life assignments seem so far beyond our education, age, talents, gifts, resources, and even our network. Marketing guru, Seth

Godin, responds to those roadblocks this way: "I'm calling that bluff. You can't change the world, but you can change five people. Why don't you just change five people today? Because if you change five people today, you will be able to change six people tomorrow, and then you're on your way—because most people change *nobody*. The way we change the world is with the smallest possible group. Change them. Repeat. You're probably surrounded with people who say they are holier than you or more authorized than you. But you don't need a permit to change someone. You just need to care."[8]

Serving is where it all begins. What is the key? Start small. When I start getting frustrated with my impact on the college campus where I teach, my wife Carol always reminds me: *"It's one student at a time."* Find someone who is lonely— someone hurting—shine a light on that person. Just change one. Then do it again.

Serving starts with identifying with the brokenness, loneliness, pain and needs of those God puts next to you in your sphere of influence. Those students sitting next to you in class. Your clients. Your neighbors. Your co-workers. Your peers. Your future friends, business associates, and colleagues. It begins with not serving out of guilt or duty, or with a grudge or desire to feel better about yourself, or to be honored for your well doing. It starts with simply caring.

How is this even truly possible?

I strongly believe the only way this can be consistently accomplished by us and sustained over time is when serving comes out of our desire to please and honor God, and it flows from our deep love for his son and his cross where he sacrificially and beautifully demonstrated his identification with *our* pain and brokenness.

Then, serving is not just about shining our light on others, it is about the beauty of *his* light burning deep inside us that attracts us to others and is attractive to others. Now we can begin to change the world one person at a time.

You just need to care.

SERVING CHANGES THE WORLD

because it changes others.
It's one person at a time.

CHAPTER 5
MAUI = MADE IN THE SHADE

"These Are The Days"
— Van Morrison[1]

"Uncloudy Day"
— Willie Nelson[2]

The first time I visited "Paradise" (a.k.a Maui), I had finished taking the Tennessee Bar Exam two days earlier and my wife, Carol, and I were celebrating our tenth wedding anniversary. Two very big milestones in our lives. For three years, Carol had worked her tail off as a makeup artist and stylist, spending two weeks each month in Virginia and two weeks in Nashville working on films, TV series, album cover photo shoots, commercials, and music videos, while I was a full-time law school student in Norfolk. During the six weeks leading up to Maui, without a job or any prospects, we moved all of our stuff back to Nashville, bringing $150,000 of fresh law school debt and the promise of hope reflected in the giant brown eyes of Sophia, our beautiful, blonde, one-year-old princess. The cat decided to stay behind in Virginia.

Preparing for the bar exam that summer made three grueling years of law school seem fairly lightweight. Imagine being tested on 20 different law school courses in a massive 12-hour examination over two days. Whenever that dreaded nightmare comes up in dinner conversations, I always tell friends that studying for the bar exam is like someone handing you a Bible and saying you must memorize the 31,000 verses in those 66 books of the Bible and be prepared to recall, quote the details, and apply the law from every single chapter and verse on the examination. *You have one month. Ready? Set? Go!*

The sensory perfection of Maui was a stunning backdrop to celebrate the ending of old seasons and the beginning of new seasons in our careers and marriage and to truly rest and recover. Let me take a moment to confess that I have a funky vacation addiction that continues to this day. For me, a vacation is not REALLY a vacation unless I read at least one book every day while I am away. This is some sort of weird, internal competition started by "Self-improvement Mark" that is about squeezing the most out of every moment, even when "Balanced Mark" is trying to focus on resting.

Well, that summer in Maui was different. Through the bar examination process, my brain undertook a new level of expansion and cleansing that I have not experienced before or since. For our ten days in Maui, I contentedly sat on the sand for hours at a time, with a slight smile and the warm sun on my face, staring off at the crystal blue horizon through Ray Bans, iced Kona coffee in hand, with the waves licking my toes, without ever picking up a single book from my suitcase library. I never even thumbed through a magazine or glanced at a newspaper. It was heavenly!

Carol and I returned to Maui a decade later to celebrate our 20th anniversary and to introduce our kids, Sophia (then 12) and Harrison (then 9), to the wonders of the Island. We rented an open-top Jeep and explored every inch of beach coastline during our two-week escape. Harrison and I took surfing lessons together. The four of us rode horses across the lush green hilltops overlooking the Pacific like we were part of "the Fellowship" in *The Lord of The Rings*. We watched the windsurfers fly over the waves at Ho'okipa Beach. God and I intimately experienced a very long and beautiful sunrise at Baldwin Beach Park. I talked my way into a late night, free, secret show by part-time Maui local, Willie Nelson and full band at a tiny pool hall. We scoped out all the best beaches for boogie boarding, including Makena's Little Beach, which turned out to be a clothing optional beach (oopsy-daisy).

All four of us would agree, our trip to Maui ranks #1 out of all of our Maxwell family vacations. Maui is pretty special. It is an amazing, multi-sensory experience. For those readers who have never been, let me explain just a bit more:

We savored our morning breakfasts of fresh mango from the farmer's market and Kona Peaberry coffee. Unbelievably, crazy good.

One moment we would be driving by majestic mountains under unclouded skies and the next moment through the gentle rain of tropical rainforests with the surprise fragrance of tropical flowers like plumeria and ginger.

We feasted on Opa and blackened Mahi fish sandwiches pulled out of the ocean by local fisherman just minutes before. The best fish I have ever put in my mouth. You will tear up on the first bite.

We laughed at warm ocean breezes on our faces and the sun heated to a perfect temperature on our shoulders as we made wide, carving turns along the palm-lined coastline, while Bob Marley provided a killer soundtrack.

A double rainbow? No way!

We ran to the beach every night to witness yet another spectacular, color-crashing sunset, each evening's show more magnificent than the night before.

Sounds perfect, right?

It was.

Heaven on earth.

I have never visited a place that exhibits God's creative genius and his smile toward mankind in a more impressive way than Maui. In fact, I often say that I am going to be pretty disappointed if God somehow fails to outfit Heaven with all the flawless sensory amenities we experienced in Maui.

Well, scratch the nude beach.

Back in the first century, the Greeks' vision of perfect paradise was illustrated by the island of Cyprus. The Greeks called Cyprus the "Happy Isle." They believed because of its geographical location, perfect climate, and fertile soil, anyone living there had it "made in the shade." They believed everything you needed to be happy was found on Cyprus. It was exquisite. It was the Maui of its day. And similar to Maui, it was often only enjoyed by the accomplished and successful. The term they associated with Cyprus was *makarios*.[3]

This Greek word *makarios* was the original word translated into English as *blessed*, the word that Christ used throughout his great Sermon on the Mount to describe those who would follow him. Blessed is an important word. Unfortunately, in our modern culture, this beautiful, spiritual word has been flippantly overused and weakened to make us think that it is simply an old-fashioned way of saying happy. *Happy* are those who mourn, *happy* are the meek. The word *blessed* means much more. According to New York City pastor and author Tim Keller, Bible scholars say that a better translation of the word *blessed* is our word *successful*. *Makarios* or a *blessed* or *successful* person describes one who is fortunate, accomplished, well-off, one who has lived so well that he is imitated and emulated.

Those who are our role models, celebrities, heroes! It also means a self-contained happiness: *a happiness independent of our circumstances.*[4]

Imagine Jesus, the homeless, prophet, Son of God who will give away everything on the road toward his violent death on the cross, looking down on that huge crowd from his seat on that mountain top. Why was Jesus speaking from a mountain top? Tim Keller explains: "These mountains had the very same function that mountains have had for centuries. If you were a revolutionary or wanted to bring in a new kingdom or new administration, you were a hunted man. So, you would hide out in the mountains. Just as the revolutionaries hide in the mountains, so Jesus Christ goes to the mountains: He is bringing about a revolution. He is a subversive."[5]

As he begins to give perhaps *the* most famous speech of all time[6], he pictures in his mind's eye a paradise island like Maui, where only the well-off and elite exclusively may live, rest, and soak in the fruits of their accomplishments; he prepares to use that analogy as a word picture of one who is *blessed* or *successful,* or one who has everything in life.

The crowd is quieted.

Jesus begins:

"Blessed (Successful) are the poor, for theirs is the kingdom of heaven." [*Wait, he must have meant to say 'the rich', right?*]

"Blessed (Successful) are the meek, for they shall inherit the earth." [*Wait, shouldn't that be 'blessed' are the strong?*]

"Blessed (Successful) are the persecuted, for they shall be rewarded. [*Hold on, shouldn't that be 'the popular' shall be rewarded?*]

Wait, what?

Once again, in that moment, Jesus grabs the world's definition of success *(blessed, makarios)* and stands it on its head. He replaces it with a new, upside-down definition that is a complete reversal of the world's view of success based on wealth, power, fame, comfort and recognition.

The *success* or *makarios* pathway Jesus describes in Matthew 5 for his followers is not about becoming well-off, one of the fortunate few or the envied elite; the pathway to success he taught that day is found through spiritual poverty, bearing sorrow, humility, hunger, active compassion and peacemaking, ethical purity and persecution.

Tim Keller argues that, when you live according to the world's definition of success, "you are driven by the power of the now because of its results, it's only temporary. You may laugh now, but later you'll weep. You may be filled now, but later you'll be empty. Jesus taught common sense. If you say the now is all that matters, who knows about eternity or other things? If you build your life on the now, you get results in the now, but the plain fact is that these things have to crumble eventually. If you build your life on your beauty, your beauty is going to fade. If you build your life on people who love you, they're going to die. If you build your life on achievement and power, your records will be eclipsed. Also, if the "now" isn't all there is, if there actually is an eternal world, then, of course, people who build their lives on wealth, power, fame, comfort and recognition will find their full stomachs turning into cosmic emptiness. Their laughter will turn into cosmic grief and weeping."[7]

We *must* begin to view our lives as a student, young professional, creative or business person through the lens of eternity. My pastor, Dale Evrist, refers to this daily life-orientation as having bi-focal vision. His promises are not limited to a far-away vision of paradise; we can enjoy and embrace his promises today, too. Dietrich Bonhoeffer describes Christ's current and future promise to his followers like this: "*They have their treasure in secret,* they find it on the cross. And they have the promise that they will one day visibly enjoy the glory of the kingdom, which in principle is already realized in the utter poverty of the cross."[8]

What Jesus taught that day on the mountain contradicts everything we know and all we are taught in college about success in business, career development and personal growth. It cuts against our natural tendency to promote ourselves, push our agenda and gain ground for "me." *How can sacrificial serving really be the answer? Can Jesus possibly be right?*

As we follow Christ, through his power we begin to experience a complete reversal of values. Power, fame, comfort and recognition no longer have a hold on our identity and life purposes. As Christians, our values and definition of success shift, and we begin to operate our lives under a new system. Bonhoeffer says: "The pure in heart have a childlike simplicity like Adam before the fall, their hearts are not ruled by their conscience, but by the will of Jesus. The pure heart belongs exclusively to Christ. For then their hearts…are not distracted by conflicting desires and intentions. They are wholly absorbed by the contemplation of God." Then, the promise of blessing to those "whose hearts have become a reflection of the image of Jesus Christ" is that they shall see God![8]

I want that! I want to see God.

Well, there is no way that sort of undivided heart can be accomplished in our own strength; that can only happen through the power of Christ working in us.

Tim Keller asks: *"Why is it that you and I eventually will be, according to the Bible, as rich as kings?*

Because he became poor.

Why will you and I be comforted? Because he wept, grieved and died in the dark.

Why are you and I going to inherit the earth? Because he was meek, he was like a lamb taken to the slaughter.

Why are we going to be filled? Because on the cross, he said, "I thirst."

He became empty, so that we could become filled.

Do you see it?

If Jesus Christ had come rich, laughing, strong, popular—he would not have been successful.

Why? What did he come to do?

Because he came to save us.

He took our curse.

He bore the things we deserved for all of our selfishness.

He took the penalty we deserved for the mess we've made the world.

He went to the cross and took our punishment so that we could be blessed (successful).

Here's what that means.

When I see Jesus Christ being persecuted without any self-pity, while saving me, then I can do that, too.

When I see Jesus Christ, pouring himself out for other people, people who don't even care, people who are his enemies, I can do that now.

Why?

The knowledge of what he did for me, is a blow to my selfish heart.

He took my place. And then he put me where he deserves to be—before the throne of God, accepted and beloved.

There it is.

Look at Christ, giving all of that away. Then you can give it away, too."

+ + +

A Christ-follower is secure. *He has found his true home.* Once a Christ-follower knows his standing in heaven, he can live recklessly and generously and unselfishly. Once you begin to define success by Jesus' new terms, you will become so generous that you put yourself at financial and emotional risk. You will be generous not only with your money, talent and time, but also with your heart.

We may not all get to live on Maui, but as a true follower of Christ, being successful (or blessed) is completely independent of our circumstances. So, no matter what is happening outside of us, through our faith and by following his teachings and example, we can experience a beauty similar to Maui at a much deeper level than through our five natural senses: through hope, peace and comfort in our hearts by the power and Spirit of Christ in us today and forever.

Success through serving.

Our true home now and throughout eternity.

+ + +

Below are the words of one of my favorite songs. It was written by a preacher named Josiah Atwood in 1827. The Staples Singers' version of it is a classic. It was their first hit in 1956. This is also the first song ever performed by Johnny Cash in public, as a twelve-year-old in a church. But, there is no recording of this song that will ever stick with me like Willie Nelson performing his version live, in paradise, at that surprise, secret show, late that night on Maui.

UNCLOUDY DAY

Oh, they tell me of a home far beyond the skies
Oh, they tell me of a home far away
Oh, they tell me of a home where no storm clouds rise
Oh, they tell me of an unclouded day

Oh, the land of cloudless day
Oh, the land of an unclouded day
Oh, they tell me of a home where no storm clouds rise
Oh, they tell me of an unclouded day

Oh, they tell me of a home where my friends have gone
Oh, they tell me of that land far away
Where the tree of life in eternal bloom
Sheds its fragrance through the unclouded day

Oh, the land of cloudless day
Oh, the land of an unclouded day
Oh, they tell me of a home where no storm clouds rise
Oh, they tell me of an unclouded day

Oh, they tell me of a King in His beauty there
And they tell me that mine eyes shall behold
Where He sits on the throne that is whiter than snow
In the city that is made of gold

Oh, the land of cloudless day
Oh, the land of an unclouded day
Oh, they tell me of a home where no storm clouds rise
Oh, they tell me of an unclouded day

Oh, they tell me that He smiles on His children there
And His smile drives their sorrows all away
And they tell me that no tears ever come again
In that lovely land of unclouded day

Oh, the land of cloudless day
Oh, the land of an unclouded day
Oh, they tell me of a home where no storm clouds rise
Oh, they tell me of an unclouded day

PART 4

TRASHING YOUR AGENDA AND EMBRACING YOUR LIFE ASSIGNMENTS & MISSION FIELD

Trust in the Lord with all of your heart,
And lean not on your own understanding;
In ALL of your ways acknowledge Him,
And He shall direct your paths.
— King Solomon[1]

CHAPTER 6:
"BUILD AN ARK!?!?"

*Not by might nor by power,
but by My Spirit...*[1]

"It is Well with My Soul"

Over the course of each year of my almost three decades of marriage, one of my proudest claims about my fantastic life with Carol is that I can honestly say I have been married to my wife for thirty amazing years because I got sober thirty-one years ago.

How many professionals in the music business can claim that through their work in "the biz" they got clean, sober, met their beautiful wife and found a true and lasting faith in God? That is *my* story. For me, I was directly rescued, *and* my future family was rescued, from the life of an alcoholic by a handful of business friends and recording artists at a record company called Word Entertainment. I remain eternally grateful.

I was an intern at Word during my final semester at Baylor University in Waco, TX. I had been a campus radio DJ and a huge music geek, but my career path was headed toward advertising. I wanted to create big TV commercials—Super Bowl-sized ads that people talked about. Word, on the other hand, distributed faith-based records and books.

When Jeff made me a job offer during that last semester at Baylor, I was flattered, but there was *no* way that I would stay in Waco and *no* way I would work for a "Christian" record company. I politely said, "Let me think about it." Meanwhile, I continued my job search and interviews around the country.

In hindsight, it is a supernatural miracle that Jeff could see a future version of me that had yet to be revealed. My young adult life had been marked with depression, hopelessness and insecurity. My escape and coping mechanisms were cocaine, crystal methamphetamine, marijuana, self-hypnosis, dream control, sexual adventures and lots and lots of alcohol. I hurt myself often, but sadly, I damaged others much more.

When graduation day came and I was still jobless, I decided to accept Word's offer so I would not have to keep waiting tables, but I knew I would secretly continue my job search looking for something better.

Then it happened. Within two months at Word, God transformed my life. He rescued me. I was a radically changed man. Within two years, Word had transferred me to Los Angeles; I was beginning to date Carol, and I was about to witness two miracles.

The first miracle occurred after a big week for our company at the New Music Seminar in NYC. The New Music Seminar is a three-day music festival and conference held each June. After we returned to Los Angeles, my boss and head of the label, Lynn, called me into his office. He thanked me for my aggressive promotions work in New York. Then he said, "Mark, I have some really big plans for you at our company that will require a great deal from you." I moved to the edge of my seat, but then his tone changed. "But, after watching your behavior in New York last week, I'm nervous. I think you might have a drinking problem."

A lightning bolt went through my heart. Deep down I knew he might be right. As a child, I watched my father destroy his career and our family with alcohol. I always thought I was better than that. As a new man of faith, I thought I could enjoy the social benefits of drinking in moderation without harming myself or others. I was responsible and self-disciplined. It wasn't working. I kept losing control and crossing boundaries.

In those moments, my mind was filled with a vivid "flash-forward" film of my future wife (possibly Carol) and my future home and my future unborn children. I would not repeat the sins of my father. I would not do to my family what he did to us. I could not do that.

That month I stopped drinking—forever. Lynn's words were a wake-up call. I am so thankful that he boldly risked taking that step right onto my toes. And that future movie of my family in my mind's eye made it surprisingly easy to end that part of my life. Three decades later, our home will typically have a small supply of wine and other drink for Carol and to serve our guests. I have never been tempted to sample it—not even once.

Then, the second miracle. A few weeks later, Lynn's long-term belief in me was evidenced when he promoted me into A&R. A record label A&R person serves as both a new talent scout and executive producer on album recordings. A&R is the dream job in the music industry. At the time, the Myrrh label at Word was the most prestigious and financially successful Christian record label in the music business—by a long shot. He interviewed over a dozen qualified candidates, including star record producers, industry veterans and seasoned musicians. I was none of the above. *I was a kid.* But for some reason, he picked me for the job.

This was the first of three moments in each decade of my over thirty-year career where I identified with David in the Bible. David was not qualified, trained or respected. He did not look the part. Yet, God picked him to be king of Israel over his brothers who were the trained and qualified professionals. Because of his heart to serve God and others, David was chosen. David was the anointed unprofessional. When we are chosen and appointed by God to serve, through his power (anointing), we can accomplish greater things than those with the experience, reputation and stature. God's anointing for service then reflects to others the wondrous and true nature and spirit behind our elevated abilities and surprising success.

For eleven wonderful years, Word trusted me to lead, develop and serve big-name legacy musical artists and discover and sign young up-and-coming rock bands. For a music junkie like me, it was pretty amazing. I loved counseling artists, and God gave me wisdom beyond my giftings in terms of song selection, production choices and artist development. I showed up in the office at 9:30 or 10:00 a.m. I spent many days working in recording studios in LA and Nashville and most nights at live concerts. I had an expense account. I was able to travel the world.

I was living the dream, especially for a young man.

My years at Word allowed me to creatively pursue and grow my passions for music, marketing, video, style, people and the Truth. In addition to my life being rescued, God miraculously took a job I didn't even want or appreciate and fashioned it into a life assignment and career in the music industry that was so much bigger, better and well-fitting than my limited dream of working in advertising. That is so often His way. Our dreams are so much smaller than His. It was the beginning of my life of counseling, connecting and caring for creatives. Creative people who positively impact culture.

God proved to me that He knew me better than I knew myself. In the Bible, Paul says, we are God's masterpiece. He has created us anew in Christ Jesus, so we can do the good things he planned for us long ago. Pastor Rick Warren says: "You are God's handcrafted work of art. You are not an assembly-line product, mass-produced without thought. You are a custom-designed, one-of-a-kind, original masterpiece."[2]

It is encouraging to recognize that God has spent a long time planning specialized, important assignments for each one of us that no one else can accomplish. Tim Keller says: "There are some deeds that only we can do, some hands that only we can hold, some hurts that only we can heal, because of the unique person he is making us to be."[3]

I could not have imagined a job that gave me more joy, influence, creative fulfillment, and opportunities to serve. It was perfectly planned and constructed for me. It was beautiful! King David says: "You saw me before I was born. Every day in my life was recorded in your book. Every moment was laid out before a single day had passed."[4] There is nothing that occurs in our lives that is ever wasted. The gifts, abilities, experiences and personalities he forges in us are for his beautiful purposes.

Fifteen years following my start at Word, I received the honor of serving and blessing Jeff by introducing him and his upstart independent record label to his first artist signing, a then-unknown band from Texas called MercyMe who had just written a song called "I Can Only Imagine."

In early 1992, there were rumors of Corporate closing the L.A. office and relocating us all to Word's Nashville office. Carol and I had zero interest in living in the South, a wonderful place to visit and make records, but not to live. Carol was a big city girl who had grown up in L.A. working in television and the music industry, and I had definitely found my permanent home on the West Coast. Besides, we were serious vegetarians. That would never fly in the early 90's version of "Nash-Vegas."

Many years ago, I heard a Bible teacher named Roy Hicks, Jr. ask this leading question: "Would you like to know the Three Keys to Success in Life? Number One: Live your life by assignment. Number Two: Live your life by assignment. Number Three: Live your life by assignment."

The principle he was teaching was based on this well-known proverb from wise King Solomon: "Trust in the Lord with all your heart and don't rely on your own understanding. But in all your ways look to him and he will make your paths straight."[5]

I have relied on this proverb at so many critical points in my life. Marriage, having children, job changes, relocations. You see, I steadfastly believe with my limited wisdom and understanding, I am incapable of safely making good decisions for myself, my family, and those in my care, and even more so when it comes to the big, life-changing determinations. But, I have supreme confidence in the directions and specific instructions my Father God has promised to me in this proverb.

Unlike the stubborn, foolish husband who refuses to listen to his wife's navigation instructions in the car, I determined I would not be a man who ignores the voice of God or refuses to request his wisdom for the road ahead. I want to safely arrive at the best destinations, on-time, with those who have put their trust in me. I want the ride to be smooth and drama-free, without time or emotion-wasting wrong turns, detours or setbacks. I want my passengers and I to experience success, joy and purpose in both our travels and our new destinations.

Below are my "truth" takeaways from the wise king's proverb:

- *Trust God fully.*

- *My wisdom is unreliable and incomplete.*

- *Look to God for wisdom and instructions concerning everything.*

- *As I do, I will have a more satisfying, meaningful and successful life.*

During my years at Word, this truth became real to me, and God proved himself as a promise keeper over and over. Our success in serving in life begins with saying yes to God's specific assignments. That is the launching pad. Pastor Jack Hayford says: "Rather than concocting your own ingredients and formulating your own schemes, if you leave the planning to Him, your days will be richer in meaning and purpose."[6] When we make determinations about our career and future solely based on our preferences, gifts, talents, and dreams, we miss the designs God has for us, we limit the dreams he has for us in serving others, and we cut short the destiny he has for those under our care and influence.

The rumors of a Nashville transfer increased. I prayed. A lot.

I started looking for a job in A&R at other rock record labels in LA to avoid the inevitable.

The rumors grew. I hiked and prayed in the Verdugo Mountains. A lot.

So many of the mainstream rock record labels were trying to get into the Christian music space. I had experience. There must be a gig that will keep me in Los Angeles.

The rumors increased. I fasted. A lot.

Malibu, Hollywood and Lake Arrowhead was our vibe. We had the perfect church! And amazing friends!

I fasted, prayed and retreated to the Point Dume cliffs overlooking the Pacific Ocean!

Please God, not "The South!"

To my astonishment, in the middle of a still night in early May of that year, the Spirit of God awakened me. I sat up in bed under the moonlight.

He very clearly said: "The answer you are seeking for your next step is that you will go to law school."

What?

"I am not smart enough to be a lawyer."

"It will be by My Spirit."

"I am too old for law school."

"It will be by My Spirit."

"I can't afford to go to law school."

"By My Spirit."

That was it, as clear as someone whispering softly in the same room.

But that was not the answer to my quest for a new record company job in L.A.

I had never considered law school and really had never thought of being a lawyer. *Ever.* I mean, *ever.*

This was ludicrous. It was crazy. I was not "lawyer" material. I couldn't make it through a week of law school. I was a creative. I made records. My hair was two feet too long and I *never* wore ties.

God might as well have said: "Build an Ark!"

God had never spoken to me that clearly or that radically. But I knew for certain it was real and true.

How could I ever tell Carol about this moment with God in the moonlight? Oh *nooo!*

I was really afraid she would laugh at me. "You, a lawyer? Bahahahahaha!"

I waited three days to tell her.

So many people I meet in life have never really heard from God, or they have given up on ever hearing from God. What a shame! Somehow these Christ-followers are unwilling to believe the promises of the Bible that inform all areas of their life. Often, their first hindrance in this belief is *philosophic.* Author Richard Foster says: "The materialistic base of our age has become so pervasive that it has given people grave doubts about their ability to reach beyond the physical world."[7]

Similarly, modern culture's ever-increasing shift toward individualism and reason is obliterating the recognition of the need for divine revelation, ancient wisdom and authority outside of one's self. *Find truth within. Let your life reveal its purpose to you. Self is king. What do you feel? Discover your deepest desires and dreams and make them a reality. Listen to your life to tell you who you are. I hustled—I conquered.*

In the immortal words of Bob Dylan: *"How does it feeeeellllll?"*

In modern culture, personal identity and purpose are no longer found by sacrificing our individual desires for the good of the family, others and society. "Instead," Tim Keller says, "we become ourselves only by asserting our individual desires *against* society, by expressing *our* feelings and fulfilling *our* dreams regardless of what anyone says." But there are flaws with this philosophy. "It assumes that our inner desires are... harmonious," says Keller. The media and our culture encourage us to identify our dreams and desires and pursue them—but those dreams often contradict one another. A particular job may conflict with deep desires for marriage and family. And our feelings often shift and change so an identity constructed on feelings will be shaky and uncertain.[8]

"Plus, an identity based independently on your own feelings is impossible—it is an illusion," says Keller. We cannot validate ourselves. We all need someone outside of ourselves to affirm our worth, to authenticate us. We all need to find our identity solely in God and let the voice of God be the One to affirm us and direct us."[9]

This modern process of self-identity creation and finding your life assignments internally can be destructive. *You must discover your dreams and fulfill them, or you are a failure.* In my work in the entertainment industry, positive things like beauty and fitness, style, chart success and positive reviews can become mandatory identity factors for young creatives. All the pressure to succeed then falls on the artist's shoulders. That is too heavy. I prefer to put the pressure of success and purpose in life on the promises of God.

The second hindrance to listening to God is *practical.* So many people either do not know how to practice the spiritual disciplines, or they are simply too lazy, busy or self-focused to take the time to develop a daily, intimate, spiritual life and friendship with God.

Instead of waiting on the voice of God, many Christ-followers plod ahead and create their own dreams and assignments based on their selfish desires and preferences. And then they pray for the blessing of God on their efforts. Activist and U2 vocalist, Bono, says: "Stop asking God to bless what you are doing. Find out what God is doing. It's already blessed."

Don't trust your preferences. Trust his promises. Don't trust your gifts and inclinations. Trust his gifts and power in you. Don't just trust what others identify for your life. Trust the voice of God and his assignments. A successful life is not about living our dream. It's not only about God's dream for us, either. A successful life is about God's dream for others through us. It's *serving.*

Other Christ-followers too quickly fade and give up on hearing the voice of God, defaulting to a flawed, superstitious game of "open" and "closed" doors. I imagine you have heard a friend say, "I never really did hear from God about it, but since 'the door' opened, I am going to trust that God opened this opportunity for me," or "I really don't know or understand God's heart on this matter, but since 'the door' closed, I will assume that was God's way of saying no." The problem with this philosophy of hearing God is that many of us have the gifts, personality, or charisma to open all kinds of doors, without that opportunity being God's assignment for us. And sometimes a "closed" door might simply be the first notice that God desires for us to fight and believe in faith for his promise that might take a little longer than what we prefer.

I have found that cultivating intimacy and two-way communication with God is really no different than intimate communication with a spouse or close family member. It simply requires sacrifice, honor, trust, heartfelt listening, love, consistency and time. Sadly, so many Christ-followers seem unwilling to make that kind of personal investment.

The disciplines of the spiritual life, like studying the Bible, prayer, solitude, worship, community and fasting, all have their important place. A great practical resource on the spiritual disciplines is Richard Foster's classic book, *Celebration of Discipline: The Path to Spiritual Growth.* "In one important sense," says Foster, "the spiritual disciplines are not hard. We need not be well advanced in matters of theology to practice the disciplines. Recent converts—for that matter or people who have yet to turn their lives over to Jesus Christ—can and should practice them. The primary requirement is a longing after God. 'As the deer longs for streams of water, so I long for you, O God. I thirst for God, the living God,' says the psalmist."[10][11]

Deep hunger. Deep thirst. Deep longing.

One of the most effective ways I have learned to hear the voice of God is by embracing solitude on personal retreats. I typically spend one to two days alone with God every January at a cabin. In addition to January, I have also spent lengthy times discussing important life decisions and changes with God on beaches, coastal cliffs, mountainsides and forest trails. I have sat and walked alone with him in the warm sun, rain, snow, sunrise and sunset in each of those beautiful settings. Just to paint an accurate picture, those hours with him include whispered words of devotion, passionate pleadings, long listening silences and loud shouting matches. Those getaways have been anywhere from six hours to several days. Jesus modeled that pattern of escape to enjoy and develop intimacy with God, and for me, imitating that habit has changed my life. And God *always* speaks.

Over the years, I have challenged many peers and young people to do the same. If you are having trouble hearing from God, I recommend that you unplug completely, go into solitude with him somewhere in his creation, and talk with him. And most importantly, listen. Just to be clear, I am talking about a significant time investment, not an hour in the morning. As men, we often take our wives on three-day weekend vacation getaways to show her our love, to grow in our friendship and intimacy, and to celebrate our lives together. Why would we not do the same with God? And we wonder why we can't hear him clearly.

"The disciplines of spiritual life call us to move beyond surface living into the depths. They invite us to explore the inner caverns of the spiritual realm. They urge us to be the answer to a hollow world," says Foster.[12] In order to serve others, we must be deep and intimate with God. We must learn to listen to His voice. One of the greatest ways we can serve others is by praying for them, which is more about listening to God than talking to Him.

"Attuning ourselves to divine breathings is spiritual work, but without it our prayer is vain repetition," he continues. Listening to the Lord is the first thing, the second thing, and the third thing necessary for successful intercession (prayer for others). Soren Kierkegaard once observed: "A man prayed, and at first he thought that prayer was talking. But he became more and more quiet until in the end he realized prayer is listening. We must hear, know, and obey the will of God before we pray it into the lives of others. The prayer of guidance constantly precedes and surrounds the prayer of faith."[13] [14]

When I told Carol about God's late-night law school assignment, fortunately for me, she did not laugh. Just the opposite. She began to passionately pray with me in faith. We began to share this crazy assignment with our pastor and with other close friends whom we knew we could trust to also hear the voice of God on our behalf. This small community of faith strengthened us and assured us, especially when some thought I had lost my marbles and others flat-out discouraged it in light of my current music business career success. A community of faithful Christ-followers surrounding you is a vital key to hearing God's voice clearly and to confidently step into his various life assignments for you.

✝ ✝ ✝

God sometimes speaks in a whisper that can change the whole course of your life.[15]

I was 33 years old. I was standing wearily in the front yard of our 1920's rental home beside a jam-packed moving truck with a tow trailer carrying my Alfa Romeo Spider convertible (think Dustin Hoffman in *The Graduate*), while Carol slid into our crystal blue boxy 1992 Toyota Land Cruiser with the cat. Three dozen close friends who helped us stuff the truck gathered around our vehicles as we were about to begin the 22-hour drive to Virginia Beach for law school. We knew no one in Virginia. We were leaving every friend we had, and it felt like we were sacrificing everything. Carol's young career as a makeup artist and stylist was exploding. What now? I had resigned from my job at Word a few weeks earlier. We did not know if we would ever return home. We were afraid. It *really* hurt.

In those days, I believe God wanted to bring Carol and me to a place where we gave him everything of our lives. Nothing held back. "The Lord wants to rid us of our fearful desire to protect ourselves, that sense of self-preservation that lurks in our hearts," says Jack Hayford.[16] "When God calls you to do His will, He may very well wrench you away from that which is familiar to you—that which causes you to build your security upon things you know, rather than upon what you know of Him."[17]

Carol made it very clear to me. This was not her preference. She did not want to go. She was not happy about it. And I was not sure if I really wanted to do it, either. I was scared. But we both confidently knew it was God's voice and assignment. We were not sure where it would all lead. But somehow, he would use it to serve others. We would obey him. And he would take care of us. In those days, Moses' negotiation with God came to mind. In Exodus 33, Moses says to God: *'If your presence doesn't take the lead here, call this trip off right now. How else will it be known that You're with (us) in this? Are You traveling with us or not? God replied, "I will personally go with you, Moses, and I will give you rest -- everything will be fine for you."*[18]

We knew God was with us.

And for you, here is a reminder for you on your assigned journey:

God is with you.

Hayford continues: "Friend, it is the easiest thing in the world to go only as far in the will of God as those around you want you to go. To advance as far as they advance. To stop when they stop. To coast when they coast. To be satisfied when they are satisfied. The Lord's call is to *you*. The people around you may or may not feel comfortable and easy about where he's calling you to go and what he's calling you to do. But it's the Lord to whom you must answer, and he is the One who not only knows the end from the beginning, he knows you better than you know yourself."[19]

I started the moving truck and Jim and Kim leaned in through the window and handed me a beautiful handmade, painted card. Below are the song lyrics on that card. I could barely read them through my tears as Carol and I pulled away.

> *When peace, like a river, attendeth my way,*
> *When sorrows like sea billows roll;*
> *Whatever my lot, Thou hast taught me to say,*
> *It is well, it is well, with my soul.*
> — Horatio Spafford (Hymn from 1876)

CHAPTER 7

FATHER'S DAY

"Redemption Song"
— Bob Marley & The Wailers[1]

"Forever Young"
— Bob Dylan[2]

I vividly remember the day my daughter, Sophia, returned home to Nashville from the Amazon. She was a beautiful, 19-year-old princess. Her shining smile and huge mane of blonde hair bouncing wildly as she ran into my arms was a moment I had been rehearsing every day for six months. I hugged her hard and held her as tight as I could without letting go. My plan that weekend was to not let her out of my sight and to keep my arm around her shoulders most of the time. Sophia had committed the past six months to train and serve as a photography missionary with Youth With A Mission. She spent the summer at a base at the mouth of the Amazon River in northern Brazil. Her international team was made up of 19 young adults ages 18 to 30 from all over the globe. Germany, New Zealand,

China, Brazil, the Dominican Republic ,and even the great Republic of Texas were each represented.

Each week, Sophia and her team traveled several hours by boat to spend time serving in a different river village with a unique people group. In addition to all of her camera gear, she boated into the jungle steam with her ENO hammock and mosquito net to hang wherever they found cover. Many nights her team slept under shelters without walls. She was cautioned to avoid getting out of her hammock for nightly bathroom breaks due to the likelihood of stepping on tarantulas! In addition to slaying giant, hairy spiders, Sophia and her team members preached, led worship and gave their time and hearts away to many river families and children. I am a proud Father!

For most of the summer in the jungle, Sophia was without cell phone service and Wi-Fi, so Carol and I had to stand strong in the silence on our end, trusting in faith in the One who had summoned her to South America and knowing her assignment to serve others and light the darkness was going to succeed. Out of her obedience, God gave her supernatural strength, boldness and influence to bring love and life to the lowest, the poor and the overlooked. Even after just a few hours with her, it was immediately evident Sophia had returned to us stronger, resilient and more open, selfless, and sensitive to others. The bug bite scars on her ankles will always remind her of those special Amazon people and the One who traveled closely by her side down the Rio Amazonas into those dark jungle nights. I am thankful for God's protection.

When Sophia was barely 16, she came to me with a specific plan:

"Dad, I really think I am supposed to go to Africa on a mission trip. I want what God did in you in Africa to happen to me as well."

Boy, I wanted that for her, too.

Soon after, I learned through Facebook that Lauren, one of my Belmont students, was strategizing a photography outreach project in Uganda with a Nashville Methodist church group led by a warm, Ugandan pastor named David. Due to poverty and the death of his father, David's mother released her son into the African Children's Choir in Uganda when he was a little boy. David eventually made his way through the American education system, which included ultimately receiving a doctoral divinity degree from Nashville's Vanderbilt University. In addition to being a Missions Pastor, David now heads Raise the Roof, a non-profit offering educational opportunities in the Ugandan villages of his childhood. Lauren was excited to mentor Sophia, and David lovingly embraced her, too. Lauren and Sophia had the honor of photographing families who had never seen pictures of themselves, and then presenting these families with framed portrait gifts. While capturing the smiles and hope in the villagers' eyes on film, the two of them were also able to capture the hearts of so many beautiful African families. And, the Africans truly captured Sophia's heart, too.

Fourteen months later, Sophia was in Africa serving with a small team from our church in a leper camp in Mombasa, Kenya. Sophia took what she learned from Lauren and David and created her own photography outreach in the Mombasa villages. Sophia's smile, joy and caring heart for the Kenyans shattered walls and brought her close and intimate with so many families and children. Her leader told me stories of children running behind the vehicle arriving with Soph into their villages, screaming, "Sophia! Sophia!" Nine months later, another young missionary we love named Kristi returned from a trip to the Mombasa camp and said all she heard was, "How is Sophia? We miss Sophia!"

The insecurities, fears and self-focus that plagues the lives of so many teenage girls were a heavy part of Sophia's young adult life, too. With all her international trips, we have watched God help Sophia strip and toss those debilitating weights aside. Sophia is learning to clearly hear the voice of God in all her decision-making and to trust him to reveal each life assignment at the proper time. Sophia has learned to die to her preferences, people-pleasing and second guessing, and to give her life away and care deeply for others. As she has served, Sophia has transformed into a mature, secure woman before our very eyes. It has been amazing to watch. She has changed.

Carol and I cannot wait to see what God has up next for Sophia! Her brief years as a photographer and missionary have been remarkable. Meanwhile, it is reassuring as a parent to know Sophia is learning that meaning for her life is not about finding her passion. In the classic, *Man's Search for Meaning,* Viktor Frankl describes this alternate ethos in this way, "It did not really matter what we expected from life, but rather what life expected from us."[3] *The New York Times'* David Brooks adds to Frankl's insight, "It's what is put in front of your path. It's not, what I want in life, but what does life want from me. It's not, what's the purpose of my life, it's what is the purpose of what's been assigned. The purpose is not to find yourself, it's to lose yourself."[4]

The secret of life is not about finding yourself; it is about losing yourself.

What is God's next assignment for you?

What does he want from you?

✝ ✝ ✝

Our family kicked off New Year's 2009 by having my 24-year-old niece, Melody, from Newport Beach, move into live with us in Nashville: indefinitely. Well, she always insisted it was just for a few months, but we always knew it would be for at least a year. We were all excited about this new adventure with Mel. Soph was 12 and Harrison was 9. So, they immediately gained a big sis, and for the first time in 17 years, Carol and I had a blood family member living in the same city with us. As a three-year-old, Melody had been our flower girl in our Malibu wedding, and unfortunately, with our escape from Los Angeles to Nashville in the early 90's, we had watched her grow up 2000 miles away. But, even with that distance and some occasional visits, we always had a special connection with Melody; she was a kindred spirit.

Unbeknownst to me at the time, in less than 60 days from the start of 2009, I would be flying into Nairobi, Kenya, for that life-changing trip.

I began those first few days of 2009 in seclusion on my yearly personal retreat at a lake house. During those days, God gave me a puzzling personal theme for 2009 based on my study of his encounter with Abraham, the father of faith. Throughout the Bible and history, God repeats his fatherly propensity for changing people's names and giving them a new identity to match their new name. He so often sees our *true* identity way before we can see it for ourselves. And, when he calls us by this new name, he simultaneously releases us into new and greater purposes and assignments.

The key moment God had with Abraham ended like this: "What's more, I am changing your name. It will no longer be Abram. Instead, you will be called Abraham, for you will be the Father of many nations. I will make you extremely fruitful

(Genesis 17:5-6)."[5] *Abram* meant *Father,* but God said there was more. Now he would be called *Abraham.* God added *his* name to the end of Abram to symbolize a multiplication of sons and daughters, a great legacy, a nation that would change the world. By imparting a portion of his name, God associated the patriarch more nearly to himself; a deep intimacy and identification was being offered to Abram in that moment. Abraham would be *near* God, and Abraham would be *like* God.

I wrote this entry in my journal that day: *Me—Father— Like God. Genesis 17:5 "Father"—fruitful, nations, kings.* I was a father to Sophia and Harrison at that time, which was such a beautiful responsibility, but I sensed God was also saying to me there was more. Okay…maybe this had something to do with Melody becoming part of the Maxwell family that year. I really did not know. But, God's stamp was strong and clear during my retreat. At the risk of sounding presumptuous, even though I did not really understand what it meant, I returned home with the word "Father" as a personal summons to me in a similar sense to that night when God pulled Abraham in close to his breath and said you will be like and near me.

At a very young age, Melody lost her birth father (Carol's brother, Dan) to divorce and decades of drug addiction. Her stepfather, Wayne, had wonderfully filled the father role for Melody for many years, but recently things had shifted again with a fresh loss when he also divorced Melody's mother.

As we began to get to know the adult version of Melody that year, we began to love her very deeply. She was a beautiful, adventurous young woman. She was full of fire and would squeeze every drop of life out of each day. We also began to get to know the real Melody. The one that she didn't show others once she walked out the front door. We began to understand her heartbreak from broken promises, inconsistency, and the absence of peace in her home and childhood. We were determined to bring loving redemption to those specific areas that had been breached in her life.

Early that year, I invited her to go with me to hear Marc Broussard at a live in-store performance at Grimey's Records and to grab a coffee at Frothy Monkey to chat afterward. She later told me how surprised she was that I wanted to spend time with her. That was something new. I began to spend specific weekly times connecting with her and praying for her. We rarely missed them. We talked about her dreams, her fears, her past, and her hopes. And we talked about God, music, songwriting, justice and Bob Dylan (of course.) And I would invite her to join me for different live music events from time to time.

God gave me a supernatural compassion for her, a grace that turned my heart toward her with the love of a father. I remember realizing and writing in my journal that: "Melody needs to understand the Father's love for her." There is a beautiful, modern hymn that describes it perfectly, called, "How Deep the Father's Love for Us." If I could model that in some small way, I knew there would be healing and growth for her. I would be present. I would be available. That is the character of God. That is how Jesus lived and served others.

Bob Goff says, "I learned that faith isn't about knowing all of the right stuff or obeying a list of rules. It's something more—something more costly because it is about being present and making a sacrifice. Perhaps that's why Jesus is sometimes called Immanuel—'God with us.' I think that's what God had in mind, for Jesus to be present, to just be with us. It's also what he has in mind for us when it comes to other people."[6]

One of the greatest expressions of love and serving comes through our time with others. Rick Warren says, "Time is your most precious gift because you only have a set amount of it. You can make more money but can't make more time. When you give someone your time, you are giving them a portion of your life that you will never get back. Your time is your life. That is why the greatest gift you can give someone is your time."[7]

During February of that year, Pastor Dale Evrist was teaching a Bible series out of The Gospel of Mark called "The Servant on the Move." He challenged us with this question: "How can we out-serve each other in our homes? Our homes need to be a place where people can come for life, power and love. We have self-imposed limits to our serving. We need to be willing to be inconvenienced, to be uncomfortable, to sacrifice, to be rejected and embarrassed."

We had a long way to go. But, with Melody's arrival, the doors to our home and our hearts were now oiled and beginning to move. The Maxwells' rusty old patterns of guarding our weekends and family time and our "me" times were beginning to shift. God was showing us new ways to serve that were about our home, and family, and intimacy. Being present, available, and unprotected. The beautiful gifts and blessings God gives us are never just for us, including our home and family. Every gift from him is designed to be shared with others, to serve their needs, to heal their hearts and to help them know how deep the Father's love is for them.

✝ ✝ ✝

Fall had arrived a few days early. The weather was perfect. Crisp sunshine without the heat. The two of us stood alone in still isolation at the front of the Leiper's Fork, TN, country home by a peaceful fishing pond covered in lily pads. It was now "magic hour"—that last hour of sunlight in a day—perfection for photographers. One hundred and fifty friends and family members were seated behind the house in front of the barn with their backs facing away from the two of us. They patiently waited to see her beauty unveiled that afternoon. Her fiancé and his mustachioed crew in yellow suspenders and high-water gray pants nervously shuffled their feet. It did not matter. This was her day. She could take as long as she wanted. We waited. We listened to the music play. We listened and waited some more. I had already offered her my left arm. She held on tight and leaned in close beside me. Every prayer had already been said.

Morgan looked radiant. Beautiful.

She wore an elegant, off-the-shoulder, classic dress and she held a bouquet of wild flowers. Her hair was loose and flowing.

I looked down into her eyes. I am 6'1" and she is not even 5-feet.

"How are you feeling?"

"Good, how about you?"

Her eyes were soft and peaceful.

"Oh, I'm fine. This is going to be a beautiful day for you, Morgan. I am so happy for you. I am so proud of you."

"Thank you."

"You are going to be a great wife," I whispered.

God was there.

"Let's enjoy our walk. Slowly, ok?"

And we did.

As we paced toward the rising, smiling, glowing faces, I was amazed at the journey Morgan and our family had been allowed to share. It was a true gift.

This was quite a culminating moment to be asked to walk Morgan down the aisle and give her away to her groom, Grant.

To give her away.

To release her from the care of our family and give her into the care of her husband.

Morgan was 20 when we first met her, and we invited her to live with our family about 8 months after Melody moved back to California. Morgan was 21 when she moved in with us through our church internship program. We were committed to host her for one year. Her program ended. She stayed another year. And then a third year.

Not only was I invited to walk her down the aisle as her "spiritual father", I was also the man whom Grant approached to ask for her hand in marriage. What a high honor and great responsibility.

Morgan grew up in Northern California. She has never met her birth father and her grandparents raised her after rescuing her as a toddler from her birth mother, an addict. Morgan's grandfather passed away while she was living with us.

The Maxwells now had a little experience under our belts when it came to inviting others into our family and home. In between Melody and Morgan, we were honored to have two other young ladies from our church live with us—Nikki and Crystal. Both are our daughters in the faith and very dear to our family, too. A few years ago, we were honored to host

Crystal's wedding in our backyard, and I cannot imagine our lives without Nikki Murray. She is one of the most grateful people I have ever met. Since Morgan's wedding, I was also honored to walk down the marriage aisle with Jadrian, a second spiritual daughter Carol and I love. During those days, our family began to connect with a young man named JoeAngel, a much-loved son in the faith and an ongoing amazing blessing to our family. Joe has brought so much joy to our lives.

With all four of these young ladies, we made it clear that they would not be treated as tenants; they would live in our home as family. The expectations on each of them was the same as on Sophia and Harrison. Our children were expected to contribute to the management and function of the home; they would, too. Our children were expected to participate in certain family gatherings and mealtimes; they would, too. Our children were not responsible for rent, nor would they.

Adopting Morgan into our family was not easy. It was actually pretty difficult for all five of us. There were many nights where I know she was ready to bolt out the door due to deep-rooted trust issues from her past. Similarly, there were many nights where Carol and I would look at each other in the eye and say, "I don't know if we can do this." But, each time we would pray, and God would tell us our assignment was not over, and then he would give us another supernatural dose of compassion and grace for Morgan. Don't get me wrong,

Morgan became a wonderful big sister to Sophia and Harrison; we shared so much laughter and many wonderful memories, and most of the time she brought absolute joy into our lives. But, sometimes the pain and brokenness of her past led to some tough moments in our home.

Our homes need to be places where people can come for life, power and love. Our homes need to be holy sanctuaries that help to release dreams in others. "Joseph was the only son that Jacob really loved—and he was also the only one able to dream," says Wayne Cordeiro. "Coincidence? I don't think so. Something about the assurance of being loved allows a person to uncover hidden potential. Love awakened the faith to believe. In the Gospel of John, Christ reminds us that 'perfect love casts out fear.'"[8 9]

Our homes and hearts must be flooded with compassion. Compassion is the foundation for serving as a spiritual parent. In his classic study of Rembrandt's painting, *Return of the Prodigal Son,* Henri Nouwen suggests three ways toward serving and loving with the compassion of the Father: through grief, forgiveness and generosity.

Grief: "Grief asks me to allow the sins of the world to pierce my heart and make me shed tears, many tears for them. There is no compassion without many tears." When our deep understanding of a person's pain and brokenness moves from our head to our heart, we become like the Father.

Forgiveness: "It is through constant forgiveness that we become like the Father. Forgiveness from the heart is very, very difficult. It is next to impossible. I must practice divine forgiveness. It calls me to keep stepping over all my arguments that say forgiveness is unwise, unhealthy and impractical."

Generosity: "There is nothing the Father keeps for himself. He pours himself out for his sons (and daughters). In order to become like the Father, I must be generous as the Father is generous. The giving of self is a discipline because it is something that does not come spontaneously. But as children of the light who know that perfect love casts out all fear, it becomes possible to give away all that we have for others. Every time I take a step in the direction of generosity, I know that I am moving from fear to love."

"The call to become the Father," explains Nouwen, "is to say to the son and daughter: *"You are with me always!"* and, *"All I have is yours."*[10]

Recently, Morgan and Grant had their first child.

They named him Abraham.

✚ ✚ ✚

My father never met a stranger. As a little boy, I remember how he could walk into the expansive, polished office of a powerful Fort Worth millionaire businessman, shake his hand, share a joke and convince him to part with a sizable piece of his fortune for a major philanthropic or community cause. A month later, I would watch my father step from the dust and tumbleweeds in Nowhere, Texas, through a squeaky door of a roadside gas station and lovingly connect and laugh for 30 minutes with a poor, elderly African American gas station attendant. It was like they were long lost childhood best friends! Dad had the gift of instant trust and influence with everyone, without even consciously trying.

But, alcoholism and mental illness stole my father from me. I watched my 6'4" hero crumble. The pressure of life broke him in two. After an annual series of job losses, each one less prestigious and lower paying than the previous, when I was 16, he was fired for drunkenness from his latest and final job: peddling cheap men's suits for minimum wage. He never worked again. After that, he tried to escape his demons by hiding under the bed covers all day while Mom worked hard to provide for the family on a school teacher's salary.

I began a destructive path to escape the pain of his absence, my own alcoholism and drug abuse of all sorts throughout high school and college. In high school, I helped destroy several friends through drugs: two from fatal car crashes, one of whom I sold drugs to the night of his crash. Sadly, others I introduced to drugs dealt with addiction for years to come. In college, I left a long path of destruction in terms of young women's lives and hearts. I was the worst nightmare of any father with a college-aged daughter. With one instance in the girl's dorm, I was put on disciplinary probation and required to meet with the Dean of Students on a monthly basis for the remainder of my years at Baylor. I was one of the worst influences on that college campus.

After graduation, when I finally came to the end of seeking my own escape and God saved me, I remember timidly visiting several churches in my college town to attempt to connect with new young adults who were Christ-followers. They were not welcoming at all. I was not trusted due to my bad reputation. I imagine they felt like the early Christians who were instructed to love and welcome Paul, the transformed man who had previously tormented and destroyed their dearest friends and family members. I was a new man, but the spirit of God would still have to creatively prepare the hearts of others to recognize my re-birth.

When the soles of my feet first stepped onto the Belmont University campus twenty-five years later, I did not recognize the redemptive story that God was telling with this new chapter of my life. As a Belmont University professor, God has supernaturally equipped me with the words and abilities to teach a variety of music business courses. I feel his authority and power when I step onto that college campus. With each obedient step, I see God using me in the lives of students who need love, life and career counsel, truth, as well as salvation and healing from their own broken and violated pasts and their current pain. On a weekly basis, God gives me trust and great influence in student's lives *without even consciously trying.*

Before each semester begins, I study my students' names, their hometowns, and fields of study, and I begin to regularly pray for each of them individually by name, believing that each one was handpicked by God for me. As I look over their faces and into their eyes during nightly class lecture, I pray that God would freshly break my heart for them and highlight different ones who need more of my time and attention. As I try to forget about myself and stay sensitive to them, God is faithful to open up their hearts toward me and use our conversations in powerful ways.

Each week, I try to efficiently nail my law practice responsibilities so I can spend extra time on the campus. Though not required for any course, I strongly encourage each one of my students to meet with me outside of class at least once that semester, usually for coffee at Bongo Java where my vision for Belmont began. A large number of students do take me up on it, and for many, that is the start of a series of meetings we will have throughout their college days and afterward. I go into each one of those meetings believing that our conversation will be rich and deep, and that God will give me wisdom in how I can best serve that student in response to his or her needs and dreams. I listen to them intently, learn their stories, and pray in those sacred moments for less of my opinions and guesses and more of the words of God to flow through me.

When the disciples of Jesus were arguing about which one of them would be famous, the greatest and most successful, Christ responded by bringing a child into their circle close by his side. He said, "Whoever accepts this child as if the child were me, accepts me. And whoever accepts me, accepts the One who sent me. You become great by accepting, not asserting. Your spirit, not your size, makes the difference."[11] As a professor, all the lecture preparation, classroom time, and grading can be hard and time-consuming work. But, those flashes of time with young ones, nodding over coffee, eye-to-eye, building them up, is the great pay-off for all that other work.

I have always admired Abraham Lincoln's viewpoint on achieving success and leadership via extreme availability to others. His door was always open. As president, his personal secretaries recorded that Lincoln spent 75% of his time meeting with others. His leadership philosophy was that he would meet with as many people as often as he was able.[12] So many men my age spout their selfish theories on business success and life skills through carefully managing their time and limiting their access to other people. I love Bob Goff's philosophy that models President Lincoln's idea and echoes the heart of Christ: "People with the greatest influence are the ones who are most available."[13]

Sharing my life and the lives of my family with my students is always filled with joy and surprises. My family and I host student class parties each semester, along with crazy Halloween costume parties, Oscar film voting parties, and end of semester bowling nights! I'm thrilled to be introduced as a mentor and called a spiritual father, and Carol and I are proud to become "home-away-from-home" parents as long-distance partners with a student's mother and father. One of our greatest honors is to be asked to celebrate at a dinner with a student's family during graduation week and to be thanked by his or her parents for our openness and consistency with their student during the four years away in college. Post-graduation, Carol and I have even been invited to attend student weddings!

It was initially jarring, and it is still humbling, to sometimes hear my students refer to me as their best or favorite professor. My lecture and classroom skills are limited. I know any real and lasting success I have as a professor comes through deeply loving my students. Caring is the key. And I care deeply about them. And it is astounding to watch how my love and serving consistently trumps my limited experience as a lecturer and academic.

My life as a college professor has become one of the most natural and valuable assignments of serving others that God has ever given me. Remember, I initially thought that door in Kibera was leading me to serve young ones in another country on the other side of the world. Instead, God designed my new mission field only 22 miles from my doorstep in the heart of Music City, where young creatives were arriving in droves after leaving their hometowns and families. God's revelation about Abraham and becoming a father of a multitude began to make more sense. And now, when I describe my life on Belmont's campus, I often tell others I am really a missionary simply disguised as a professor.

You must see it, God is in the business of redeeming what was destroyed!

Without a father, I became a father. God truly became my Father, fixed my own self-destruction and blessed me with my own children, and he continues to multiply the spiritual children in Carol and my life each month.

Like Paul, who destroyed and imprisoned the early Christ-followers, was chosen to serve and lead the Church, God chose me to serve and lead young artists, college students, young ladies, and young men, the very people I spent so much time destroying and imprisoning when I was a young man. Twenty-five years later, I stepped back onto a university campus to bring life instead of death, truth instead of lies, hope instead of pain. I still get goosebumps when I think about it! What a beautiful picture of God's redemption.

In God's order for our lives, there is no such thing as disqualification. Your broken past does not limit the serving assignments God has planned for you. In fact, the very thing you may have destroyed in your own life *and* in the lives of others may be the *exact* areas or themes God may end up using through you to bring his redemption and restoration to others.

Look, you are not disqualified! Whether you feel like you have disqualified yourself or someone else's harm to you or absence in your life has disqualified you, *you are not!* You are a chosen vessel for Him. God can redeem it all because you are part of his redemptive plan and story. You must overlook your limited giftings, let go of your preferences, and faithfully align yourself with his purposes for you.

And then you will find your mission field!

Listen carefully:
Unless a grain of wheat is buried in the ground,
dead to the world,
it is never more than a grain of wheat.
But if it's buried,
it sprouts and reproduces itself many times over.
In the same way, anyone who holds on to life
just as it is destroys that life.
But if you let it go, reckless in your love,
you'll have it forever, real and eternal.
— Jesus Christ[14]

PART 5

LESSONS IN SERVING

X

For everything we know about God's plan for mankind
can be summed up in a single sentence:
Love others as you love yourself.
That's an act of true freedom.
— St. Paul[1]

CHAPTER 8:
"GOD, THIS WAS YOUR IDEA!"

"You Are the Sunshine of My Life"
— Stevie Wonder[1]

"Thunder Road"
—Bruce Springsteen[2]

I really never had any interest in studying law. I never dreamed of returning to any sort of graduate school program. This was outrageous. I was "Creative Music Guy" not "Legal Guy." So weird. Like Rob and Barry at Championship Vinyl in the film *High Fidelity*, my preference for a second career would have been to buy a little record shop and fritter the day away listening to music with geeks and talking about important vinyl releases: "Don't tell anyone you don't own *Blonde on Blonde*. It's gonna be okay." Going to law school and becoming a lawyer completely messed with my identity. But God confirmed his assignment again and again. A new level of humility and sacrifice was required. Law school was the hardest thing I'd ever done. I was in over my head every day for three years. But, it was healthy to be forced to daily rely on the power of God.

It felt the same way when I first opened the doors to my law practice. Pastor Dale Evrist has a great saying, "If you are not in over your head, you are probably not fully walking in God's will." That's reassuring, though it can feel slightly masochistic.

In those early days of lawyering, I was always grateful for any wisdom and advice I could receive from other seasoned entertainment attorneys. I remember requesting such a meeting with my friend, Richard, head of Legal Affairs for Capitol Records. Richard was very sharp and had been around the block. He was a serious and respected music attorney with deep Hollywood roots. He always wore black Armani suits. He and I first met ten years earlier when I was trying to hire his client, a young producer who had just produced Mariah Carey's debut album, for an album I was executive producing.

"Richard, you know, I am launching my law office this fall. I know this is a pretty general question, but I just wondered if you might have any advice for me?"

He was very kind, but a little intimidating. Sitting in the stumpy chair with his huge desk between us, I felt a little like Luke Skywalker impatiently asking Yoda for the secrets of the universe.

"Mark, the key to a successful law practice is serving. It's all about serving your clients. That's it. It is pretty simple."

I remember walking out thinking in my mind, "Sure. Of course. That's easy. Nothing new for me. Oh, yeah, some good thoughts, but I sort of thought I might receive something more profound and unique. I mean, Richard is *the man*; is that all he had for me?"

Little did I know, I still had so much to learn.

As I began to build my law practice, one of the first lessons I learned was serving my clients without relying on them, what I call *serving without reliance*. When you are starting a new business from scratch, it is really hard to predict where new clients might come from, how much work they will generate, and how often they will need your services. As a new business, it is so easy to begin to unconsciously shift away from your center of being a high-quality service-oriented business, to one that is desperately networking and recklessly driven out of fear or greed to find new business and clients.

Once you cross the boundary into those poor networking motivations, your service with existing clients becomes routine and impersonal because you are focused on who is next in line who will help you generate revenue (think Jerry Seinfeld standing before the Soup Nazi: "Next!"). Plus, your ability to win trust and confidence with potential new clients is hindered by your lack of eye contact, racing heart, insincere words and sweaty palms.

Picture standing at an industry event or convention; everyone has drinks in hand. A young man approaches you with an introduction and handshake and nervously starts a conversation, but the whole time his eyes are darting over your shoulders for someone more important who might be able to offer some immediate business opportunities. This is sick and sad, yet so common.

About five years into the launch of my practice, I was fighting financial fear. I had clients who were not paying me on time and others who were not paying me at all. I was ticked and on edge. New business was slow. My emotions were on a constant roller coaster ride that was tied to the frequency of the arrival of checks and new client engagement letters in my mailbox. I was so worried. I remember those long stressful walks to the mailbox each night believing for cash or commitments. I would open that box again and again: nothing. Empty. Pretty soon it went from not only hollow to vacant with a punch in the nose. I would open the box and imagine, just like a jack-in-the-box, a giant boxing glove on the end of a retractable spring would punch me hard right in the face, just like Daffy Duck received in those classic Bugs Bunny cartoons.

I had entered a downward spiral of cursing my clients instead of blessing them. How do you like *that* for serving?

Out of my desperate prayers, God began to show me that I needed to deeply recognize and acknowledge that He is my provider and very specifically, that no one else is in that role. No client, no new business opportunity, no one.

God is My Provider; clients, jobs and bosses are simply channels of His provision.

God has made many beautiful promises that we can rely upon. He says: "I will never [under any circumstances] desert you [nor give you up nor leave you without support, nor will I in any degree leave you helpless], nor will I forsake you or let you down or relax my hold on you [assuredly not]!" So, we take comfort and are encouraged and confidently say, "The Lord is my helper [in time of need], I will not be afraid. What will man do to me?"[3]

And Jesus said these reassuring words: "Walk out into the fields and look at the wildflowers. They never primp or shop, but have you ever seen color and design quite like it? The ten best-dressed men and women in the country look shabby alongside them. If God gives such attention to the appearance of wildflowers—most of which are never even seen—don't you think He'll attend to you, take pride in you, do His best for you? What I'm trying to do here is to get you to relax, to not be so preoccupied with getting, so you can respond to God's giving. People who don't know God and the way He works, fuss over these things, but you know both God and how He works. Steep your life in God-reality, God-initiative, God-provisions. Don't worry about missing out. You'll find all your everyday human concerns will be met. Give your entire attention to what God is doing right now, and don't get worked up about what may or may not happen tomorrow. God will help you deal with whatever hard things come up when the time comes."[4]

I began to learn to face financial and business pressure with this new reality. Plus, when you begin to order and design your life and career with His life assignments and serving plans instead of your preferences and selfish dreams, you can put that financial and business pressure on him. To this day, when those pressures arise (and they often do), I can shout with confidence: "*God this was your idea!* This lawyer-thing and life assignment was completely your idea—it was not my dream or plan, this was your plan and assignment for my life, so it is up to you to somehow meet the financial needs for my business and family. The pressure is on you, not me. I can't emotionally bear it. I can't see the resources coming today, but you can make that happen. I can't see the new clients I desperately need, but you can send them my way. You promised!"

We are not created to emotionally bear that kind of pressure. As children of God, we don't have to shoulder it. There is a fantastic Hebrew word *galal* which describes the real rest that begins with rolling away these kinds of burdens. We can roll these cares off our shoulders on to his. "Roll your way and each care of your load upon the Lord, lean on Him, and He will help you. He will make your innocence radiate like the dawn, and the justice of your cause will shine like the noonday sun. Roll the burdens of your daily work and life upon the Lord and He will cause your thoughts to become agreeable to His will and then your plans will be established and succeed."[5]

But, going forward, how do I respond to my clients who are not paying me on time or who appear to be stiffing me on my invoices? God showed me that I must continue to serve them *more and better* with a new heart. I had to begin to bless them instead of curse them. *What? How is that?*

Out of obedience, I initiated a weekly prayer time for all my clients on Monday mornings. God prompted me to begin praying for those flaky clients regularly. I prayed for their businesses, their marriages and their personal finances. I cannot say exactly how that changed their ability and integrity when it came to paying me, but that did not matter. I know God answers prayers and He began to change their circumstances, and in some ways, even more importantly, my heart toward that group of clients began to transform, and it helped me keep my heart clean from future offenses with new clients. Now, I could stand in peace in those storms and my clean, forgiving heart allowed me to gratefully receive His promises. By faithfully continuing to serve those clients through prayer, God brought provision to both them and me.

It did not matter if my legal clients *ever* paid me, I knew *God was my sole provider.*

"We need never shout across the spaces to an absent God.
He is nearer than our own soul,
closer than our most secret thoughts."
— A.W. Tozer[6]

+ + +

"Show a little faith, there's magic in the night..."
— Bruce Springsteen

When Sophia and Harrison each turned sixteen, I took them out individually on a special night to see Bruce Springsteen and the E Street Band perform live. Neither one knows his albums like I do, but they both recognize his reputation for giving an audience way more than their money's worth and much more than any other live performer. They were each very excited to be there with me.

Before the show three years ago, Sophia and I waited in line outside the concert arena to get into the coveted general admission floor area. We struck up a conversation with a doctor who flew in from Chicago. This was his 273rd Springsteen show. Another fan claimed 176 shows. The couple beside us had flown in from Pennsylvania. This would be the 89th time they had seen Bruce live. Crazy! Sophia suddenly realized there were bigger music geeks in the world than her fanatic father! There are no current musical artists who evoke this kind of loyalty and repeat business like Bruce. Plus, there are no artists who consistently give their fans a generous three-and-a-half-hour-plus show with no break. In 2016, Bruce broke his previous record for his longest show in the United States by playing four hours and three minutes in Philadelphia. At age 66. Super-human! He makes young men look and feel old. I know how tired I am after one of his shows. I can't imagine how he and the band physically recover night after night.

Harrison and I planned our night out seeing Bruce's The River Tour in Louisville. We had our floor tickets in-hand and waited through the afternoon lottery process to see if we would be among the lucky few picked to be in the area closest to the stage. Bruce consciously plays to every single person in the arena or coliseum, including the cheap seat rafters and obstructed view seats, but everyone knows there is something magical in those first few rows where you can actually trade eye contact with the Boss and the members of the E Street Band. We made it into the pit! Right in front of the stage! Amazing!

Springsteen kicked off the night by shouting, "Are you ready to be transformed?"

"YEEEAHH!"

Bruce and the band blew Harrison's mind for 3 hours and 22 minutes while he and I were floating two inches off the ground 15 feet from the stage.

During one of his shows, Springsteen is constantly dancing, screaming, imploring, mugging, kicking, wind-milling, crowd-surfing, climbing a drum riser, jumping on an amp, and leaping off the piano. In return, the crowd participates in a display of communal adoration. Like pilgrims at a gigantic outdoor Mass—think John Paul II at Gdansk—they know their role: when to raise their hands, when to sway, when to sing, when to scream his name, when to bear his body, hand over hand, from the rear of the orchestra to the stage. "I want an extreme experience," he says. He wants his audience to leave the arena, as he commands them, "With your hands hurting, your feet hurting, your back hurting, and your voice sore!" So, the display of exuberance is critical.[7]

When Springsteen is asked "How do you do it?" he describes those supernatural breakthrough moments between him and a giant concert audience as a magic trick. "Eighty thousand rock 'n' roll fans waiting for you to pull something out of your hat, out of thin air, out of this world, something that before the faithful were gathered here today, was just a song-fueled rumor.[8] I am here to provide proof-of-life to that ever elusive, never completely believable 'us.' And then suddenly,"— he snapped his fingers— "you catch it, and then, once you do, you may not want to stop. You have to create the show anew, and find it anew, on a nightly basis. And sometimes," he concluded, laughing, "it takes me longer than I thought it would.[9] I tend to try and move to that place every night, to that moment where suddenly it's just you and the audience; everything else has kind of fallen away...time...space."[10]

"Thank you, Louisville! The E Street Band LOVES you!" As if we needed to be reminded. We slowly strolled to the parking lot with huge smiles and ringing ears. We HAD been transformed.

Why is Springsteen driven to go through all that hard work night after night? "For an adult, the world is constantly trying to clamp down on itself," he says. "Routine, responsibility, decay of institutions, corruption: this is all the world closing in. Music, when it's really great, pries that @#$% back open and lets people back in, it lets light in, and air in, and energy in, and sends people home with that and sends me back to the hotel with it. People carry that with them sometimes for a very long period of time."[11]

Bruce's faithful fans experience:

Supernatural Hope, Community and Light.

Each one of these elusive elements, Hope, Community and Light, are spiritually birthed when others are sacrificially and generously served. Boy, we all desperately need those today.

In his recent autobiography, Springsteen refers to his boyhood Catholic church as "the world where I found the beginning of my song."[12] Now, five decades later, Bruce is modeling (perhaps, unknowingly, perhaps not) God's great generosity to mankind, because God not only promises to provide, he promises to do so generously. Bruce is beautifully mirroring the power and story of God. By taking the power of the E Street Band's musical excellence and creativity (God's beautiful gift) and serving his fans with passion, abandon and extreme generosity, the atmosphere mysteriously changes. Paul says, "You can be sure that God will take care of everything you need, His generosity exceeding even yours in the glory that pours from Jesus. Our God and Father abounds in glory that just pours out into eternity. Yes!"[13] Our God meets and explosively surpasses our human needs.

AND God asks us to sacrificially serve others with that same extraordinary generosity. Paul instructed Timothy; "Tell those rich in this world's wealth to quit being so full of themselves and so obsessed with money, which is here today and gone tomorrow. Tell them to go after God, who piles on all the riches we could ever manage—to do good, to be rich in helping others, to be extremely generous. If they do that, they'll build a treasury that will last—gaining life that is truly life."[14]

How can we give more generously of our time, our talents and our resources?

Where can I start to give more extravagantly to my clients, family and friends? To my fellow students, my co-workers, my neighbors? To those in great need?

First, we must expect God to provide for us just like he promised.

As we do, let's embrace the freedom and motivation to serve others generously like God serves us.

Then, through our God-like generosity, let's believe we will see and experience hope, community and light "magically" born in the atmosphere of our world and in our relationships with those around us, that we may all experience and give "life that is truly life."

Eternal treasure.

SERVING PRODUCES HOPE.

Generosity creates supernatural results.

CHAPTER 9:
NO STRINGS ATTACHED

*Someday, and that day may never come, I will call upon you
to do a service for me. But until that day, consider this justice
a gift on my daughter's wedding day.*
— Vito Corleone (The Godfather)

"Don't Know Why"
— Norah Jones[1]

Early in my law practice, I escaped for a few days to a beautiful Tennessee State Park called Fall Creek Falls to dream and plan about growing my business. At the time, the new, big buzzword in business was "brand." It's a decades-old marketing and advertising term, but in the exciting internet age of the early 2000's, "brand" had been re-imagined to apply to individuals: "personal branding," sort of a strange, self-commodification focused on promoting and glorifying yourself. The "personal branding" mantra was: *"No matter what sort of work you are doing or service you are providing or artistic endeavor you are pursuing, you must begin to view yourself as a 'brand!' You must be laser-focused on building that*

brand and image, communicating your story. Everything is about establishing that brand, telling your story!"

I remember one business book author pushing this mission statement: "Your model should be Hollywood. Think of yourself not as a service provider but as a star."[2] Flash-forward a few years. This personal branding strategy is now commonplace with the current generation of young adults in terms of social media, the music business and creative industries; it's everywhere. And, it's a slippery slope!

"Our culture in the United States is aimed at surface over substance", says Rock Hall of Famer and 60's counter-culture icon, David Crosby, referring to the crazy popularity of certain YouTube and Instagram faces. "What did they create? Nothing. Who did they help? No one. What have they brought to society? What positive force have they been? None. Nothing. They are famous for being famous. It's all about being a celebrity."[3]

Someone like Kim Kardashian is estimated to earn $300,000 per week in social media advertising revenue.[4] But, financial success from such avenues is rare, and it's misleading a whole generation. Sadly, the hollow, Hollywood-designed personal branding goals can be way out of balance with the higher goals of serving others, deepening relationships, creating art and beauty, and making the world a better place.

Here is one branding idea from my lakeside reading that weekend that I thought was important enough to write in my journal:

"If you want to attract new clients and opportunities, you have to make yourself visible."[5]

At the time, most of my legal work was in Christian music and faith-based media, which was fine. But, I decided it was high time to develop more clients in the mainstream and independent rock music world. So, I booked a flight to Austin, Texas, for the upcoming South by Southwest Music Festival (SXSW). South By is a crazy week filled with late nights, where over 2,000 performing artists from all over the world come to play and rub shoulders with the music industry glitterati with the hope of finding greater exposure, networking contacts and record deals. I dropped about $2,000 on airfare, hotel, food and conference registration. I spent a week away from my family shuffling through the late night streets of downtown Austin, networking my tail off, shaking hands, meeting John Mayer's manager, watching cool new bands, handing out business cards, dodging drunks, smiling, shaking more hands and trading emails. And, hey, I even got to see Norah Jones make her debut live performance in a packed Indian food restaurant the week her first album released AND I got to watch The Shins play that song from the *Garden State* film soundtrack. Remember Natalie

Portman with her headphones: "You gotta hear this one song, it'll change your life, I swear."

Well, I made myself *visible*.

Then I came back home to Nashville and watched the days roll off the calendar. After all that time and money that I invested on the Austin networking trip, I did not gain *one new client*.

Zero! Not one! Nada!

God eventually called me into his room for a little Father-son chat.

"Mark, did you ever talk to me about going to Austin and this little plan of yours?"

"No, sir, I'm sorry. I did not even think about that."

"And, Mark, during your week in Austin, you met a lot of new people. Did you go with a heart to really serve those you met, or did you simply go to try and collect new clients?"

"Um, I think you know my answer, do I really have to say it?"

Two strikes.

I got spanked.

I don't know if I was ever really supposed to go to Austin or if I was supposed to pursue new rock clients that year, because I failed to get God's wisdom and counsel concerning *my* plans.

And, I made myself *visible*, but God wants us to make ourselves *available*. I missed so many opportunities to love and serve others that week, because my focus was on me, my needs and my business, not on the deep needs, brokenness and businesses of those with whom I rubbed shoulders.

SERVING CREATES VALUE:

for others and yourself.
Giving value lasts.

✝ ✝ ✝

At this point in the book, I imagine you may want to ask: "Mark, if you don't believe in networking, how do you find and develop new clients and grow your law practice?" *Good question.*

Here are my three keys for finding new business:

Number One: *Excellent service* for my existing clients. I do my very best to give my existing clients excellent, expert legal service that is completed at a fair price and in a timely manner. So many clients who have come to me over the years have left their prior attorney because they felt their legal work took way too long or they were overcharged, or both. Many over-zealous lawyers have a poor habit of majoring on the minors and nitpicking deals to death, to the point of exhausting their client or exasperating both parties who desire to enter into that new relationship. Simultaneously, the enormous pressure that law firm billing requirements places on lawyers, along with such nitpicking, leads to astronomical invoices. My goal is to create a client relationship built on trust and respect, where they feel valued and receive value. Once a client experiences a servant-oriented relationship that exceeds his expectations or blows up his stereotype about lawyers, that client is going to start talking about me with his contacts. And there is absolutely no better way to market my business and find new clients than when my current clients share my name with others needing legal services.

Number Two: *Through genuine love, interest and concern for others who are not my clients.* It's difficult for all of us to make time for others, and it's even harder to really care and be interested in the details of their lives. We are all busy and we all have family, school and business responsibilities that crowd out those extra moments of margin. Over the years, I try to regularly make the effort to reach out to old and new friends for a personal touch and lunch. I pray and ask the spirit of God to bring to mind someone who needs encouragement or a listening ear. I will typically buy their lunch and really try to make the conversation about them and their life, with very little business discussion. My goal is to make our encounter a no-strings-attached experience. My heart's desire is to avoid seeking business from them or to expect a business referral in return for lunch. If I feel my heart is leaning otherwise, I will not request the meeting.

So much of the networking mindset is supported by the concept of a win/win transaction. As long as both parties ultimately gain, the initiation of any sort of self-focused business interaction is justifiable. However, my experience of coming up empty-handed after Austin has repeated itself enough times that I know it is difficult for God to bless my life and business encounters when they are self-focused or when such meetings have strings attached—expecting something in return from giving. Christ modeled a life where he gave everything away, including his life, while expecting nothing in return from us. It was not a transaction or bargaining tool; there were no strings, and there was no *quid pro quo*. Christ sacrificed everything out of complete obedience to God so he might have an intimate relationship with us. As a Christ-follower, our approach to all of our relationships, including our business relationships, must be considered and evaluated through that standard.

This is difficult stuff. "Unfortunately, a lot of our service is self-serving. We serve to get others to like us, to be admired, or to achieve our own goals. That is manipulation," cautions Rick Warren.[6] Serving without expectation requires levels of humility that are not easily acquired. We are all basically steeped in selfishness, so we must constantly practice, fail, and practice again, thinking more about others than ourselves.

Number Three: *Through humility.* Thanks to C.S. Lewis, I fear pride for even acknowledging it. Lewis describes a truly humble person this way: "He will not be thinking about humility: he will not be thinking about himself at all."[7] We must constantly monitor and ask God to recalibrate our own hearts. Tim Keller reacts to C.S. Lewis' quote this way: "The thing we would remember from meeting a truly gospel-humble person is how much they seemed to be totally interested in us. Because the essence of gospel-humility is not thinking more of myself or thinking less of myself, it is thinking of myself less. Gospel-humility is not needing to think about myself. Not needing to connect things with myself. It is an end to thoughts such as, 'I'm in this room with these people, does that make me look good? Do I want to be here?' True gospel-humility means I stop connecting every experience, every conversation, with myself. In fact, I stop thinking about myself."[8]

As we humbly focus our attention on others instead of ourselves, God promises to elevate us into positions of honor and service without relying on traditional networking and slimy self-promotion. "Therefore humble yourselves under the mighty hand of God [set aside self-righteous pride], so that He may exalt you [to a place of honor in His service] at the appropriate time, casting all your cares [all your anxieties, all your worries, and all your concerns, once and for all] on Him, for He cares about you [with deepest affection, and watches over you very carefully]."[9]

How do we live and stay in a place of such humility and self-forgetfulness? There's only one way. Our hearts must stay set on pleasing God, staying obedient to his ways. We must delight in aligning our daily lives and daily moments with his teachings and his broken heart for others. As we do, his power in us, not our will power, enables and equips us to live a life beyond ourselves. That's it.

One of the interesting things about those random lunch invitations is, inevitably, six months or sometimes one year later, I get a phone call where the voice on the line says, "Mark, you don't know me, but so-and-so (the person I took to lunch) gave me your number and said you are the perfect person to help me with my legal needs." This sort of phone call happens over and over for me. When I simply live life by trying to be a good friend and trying to care for others instead of self-promoting or looking for a networking opportunity, God sneaks up on me a year later and surprises me with a new client or business opportunity connected to that distant lunch meeting.

Being human always points, and is directed, to something or someone, other than oneself—be it a meaning to fulfill or another human being to encounter.
The more one forgets himself—by giving himself to a cause to serve or another person to love—the more human he is.
— Viktor Frankl[10]

✝ ✝ ✝

One day, I was surprised to receive an email from Joe, one of the owners of one of my favorite rock music magazines. I was excited! I had been a huge fan and subscriber since their debut issue years earlier. He said he was coming to Nashville later that week, and he would like to sit down and have lunch with me to talk about legal representation. Wow, great!

When he and I met, we excitedly shared our common love for so many musical artists and records and discovered we had a dozen mutual friends. We really connected. At the end of our two-and-a-half-hour lunch, he asked if I would consider beginning to provide legal representation for his magazine. I was flattered. I thought to myself, there is no way I could have orchestrated this meeting on my own if I tried. Before we left the table, I said: "Joe, I have to ask you, how did you get my name? Who referred me to you? I really want to thank them."

He pulled my business card out of his wallet. It was bent and scratched. He said, "Well, I have been carrying your card around for two or three years. I think so-and-so gave it to me."

"I don't know who that is."

"Oh, then it must have been so-and-so.

"I have never met him, either."

"Really? That's weird. Well then, I don't know."

Joe and I never did figure out who actually referred me

to him or who gave him my business card. But, I was pretty sure, somewhere along the way when I was not networking or scrounging for business, someone at the end of a lunch meeting asked for my business card so God could supernaturally astonish me with a one-of-a-kind, handcrafted gift three years later.

✝ ✝ ✝

My first law office in 1999 consisted of a beat-up library table in a tiny cubby in the kitchen of our 1940's duplex. I was set up with an original gumdrop-shaped Bondi-blue iMac G3 and a single cardboard banker's box. One of my clients in those early months was my pastor, Dale Evrist. He had been a prime encourager of my return to law school and my second career. Pastor Dale had recently been offered a literary publishing agreement and needed a lawyer to negotiate its terms. Most of my experience in the entertainment industry up until that point had been limited to the music industry. Book contracts were new.

I offered to review and negotiate his book agreement for free. I knew this would be a wonderful opportunity to serve and bless my pastor. I took his contract very seriously. I was not going to mess around. I also saw this as a great learning experience that would force me to get up to speed on the business and contractual terms of book publishing deals so I could begin to serve other authors. I quickly bought and read three different books on book publishing agreements, one written by a literary agent, one by an entertainment attorney, and one by an academic. Then, I asked a dear entertainment attorney friend and mentor, Randy, who had negotiated many book deals, if I could buy him lunch and walk through about two dozen questions I had on the ins and outs of book contract terms. He was gracious and helped immensely.

I was confident and ready to go. We were able to negotiate and successfully close Pastor Dale's agreement with no drama.

A few months later, I was having lunch with a manager friend in Nashville. It was casual. At the end of lunch, he spun a contract across the table to me.

"Mark, I want you to represent my author-client in this new book deal he has been offered."

I was dumbfounded, but somehow played it cool. At the time, his author-client was the top seller in the Christian book market. Millions and millions of books sold. He was loved and respected. His author could easily afford to hire a seasoned, DC-based literary property attorney who represents the politicians and TV talking heads at $900 an hour.

In regard to literary publishing deals, I instantly went from zero to one hundred, and my law practice was less than a year old.

✝ ✝ ✝

In 2010, I received a call from one of the true legends and patriarchs of Nashville's music industry. This man had successfully steered the lengthy careers of several superstars and had developed many amazing artists and songwriters for decades. He founded and sold several record companies over the years. With all of his financial success, he was one of those guys who I always thought would have retired by age 40. He didn't. Oh well, he must really love working with creatives and making music too much to fade from the scene.

Before meeting him for lunch at his temporary office (California Pizza Kitchen) that day, I had heard rumors of recent hard times he had been facing. We drank coffee. He leaned back, brushed his hair back and began to explain a number of music business contracts that he needed help drafting and negotiating. Okay, the financial rumors I heard must not be true. Well, of course not; he was one of the most successful men I had ever known. Now, I was really encouraged! After all, he could afford to hire any entertainment attorney in town, even those whose hourly rates were three times mine. I was so honored that he chose me out of that long list.

Then he continued. He began to explain how the changes in the music industry along with the recent economic crash had decimated his portfolio of real estate properties and other investments. In fact, he was now trying desperately to avoid bankruptcy. Woah.

What I was hearing could not be true. But it was!

In those moments, I went from admiration to broken-hearted then back to admiration. It was clear that the thread that had sustained him during the prior two-year downward spiral was his faith in God. That was all he had. What a ride he had been on.

He humbly asked if I would be willing to begin to do some legal work for him. He was not sure when he could pay me. He had a plan he was developing to launch a new company with an investor. He had high hopes. He said if I could jump in and work for him with some flexibility and risk today, he would be loyal to me when this new company began. We tossed around reduced rates and extended payment plans. As a solo practitioner, that would be difficult for me, but in my mind, I agreed that afternoon to work without pay or under an extended payment plan, whatever it took. He and I would walk together during these months of faith. The Spirit of God gave me instant peace.

One year later, his new company began to take shape. He, his partner, and their new company became my most lucrative client and remained so for the next five years. Our friendship has grown deeply, his team has been a big part of my family's life, and he continues to be my greatest advocate for my legal services.

✠ ✠ ✠

You might call it *karma*, but God calls it seed-planting and harvesting. There is a spiritual principle on which you can stake your business, your relationships, your life. It is trustworthy and never fails. It's foolproof. It is not "pie in the sky" hope, it is real! As we generously plant and serve others, they are blessed and receive a harvest. But, that is not the end of it. Miraculously, God's spiritual accounting system also extends that harvest and blessing to us, too. Unlike any other investment you make in life, you can count on this one! There is always a good return.

The Bible says: "What a person plants, he will harvest. The person who plants selfishness, ignoring the needs of others— ignoring God!—harvests a crop of weeds. All he'll have to show for his life is weeds! But the one who plants in response to God, letting God's Spirit do the growth work in him, harvests a crop of real life, eternal life. So, let's not allow ourselves to get fatigued doing good. At the right time we will harvest a good crop if we don't give up or quit. Right now, therefore, every time we get the chance, let us work for the benefit of all, starting with the people closest to us in the community of faith."[11]

Practically, for me as an entertainment attorney, that might involve offering a free couple of hours of research or legal work, or maybe a whole day's worth of free legal work. It could be providing a job referral or a creative connection. It might be spending time with a young creative's songs or recordings and providing that person with specific feedback. It might be recommending a specific business book, contractual resource, or article to a friend or client. It might mean treating a young creative businessperson to coffee and just speaking hope and life to his or her business plans and dreams.

God asks us to stretch and give generously of our time, gifts and resources to everyone we meet: the poor, the wealthy, our friends, our classmates, our clients.

Give and keep on giving.

Serve and keep on serving.

Love and keep on loving.

Every day.

God's return and harvest is guaranteed.

SERVING CREATES PROVISION—

for others and yourself.
It flows both ways.

Invite some people who never get invited out,
the misfits from the wrong side of the tracks. You'll be—and
experience—a blessing. They won't be able to return the favor, but
the favor will be returned—oh, how it will be returned!—at the
resurrection of God's people.
— *Jesus Christ*[12]

CHAPTER 10:
"HELLO, I'M JOHNNY CASH."

You never really understand a person until you consider
things from his point of view...
Until you climb inside of his skin and walk around in it.
— Atticus Finch

"Man In Black"
— Johnny Cash[1]

"Hello in There"
— John Prine[2]

The band piled into my rental car and we nervously left Nashville that Sunday night in March to head a few miles north into Hendersonville, TN. In my car was Austin-based Christian punk band, One Bad Pig, along with their leather, chains, studs and earrings. The band had a powerful assignment serving and loving teenagers in the Austin punk club scene. A young, ordained pastor nicknamed "Kosher" was their lead singer. I still lived in Los Angeles, but we were in Nashville where I was overseeing the recording of their new album. We had been invited to a big, private birthday party where there would be no one we had ever met before. This would be very interesting.

We left the freeway and headed down some rough and dark country roads, eventually arriving outside the Bell Cove Club on the banks of Old Hickory Lake. We could hear a live band playing and lots of laughter coming from inside the building. We walked up to the door and burst right through.

Every eye in the room shifted to stare us down. We were a sight. Me and my two-foot-long bush of hair and trendy Hollywood clothes and the punk band in their dirty and decadent garb. We scanned the room. It was filled with Nashville country music legends and elite, and a handful of other country wannabes. Over there is Bill Monroe—the father of bluegrass music. There's what's-his-name, that guy from the Oak Ridge Boys with the killer beard. Everyone was there. The band on stage did not pause. Right in the middle of the packed room sat Nashville royalty—Johnny Cash and his beautiful wife, June Carter Cash—both glowing, laughing and thoroughly enjoying themselves. We caught Johnny's eye—that was not hard. Woah.

Boy, were we out of place. We stumbled along the front of the bar trying desperately not to look too noticeable. It didn't work. It felt like any moment a couple of these cowboys who thought we crashed the party might punch us in the jaw, grab us by our belts and run us out the back door for a good whipping.

Fortunately, Johnny's publicist and personal assistant, Hugh Waddell, spotted us, welcomed us in, and found us a back table to settle into. Whew.

This was Johnny and June's son John Carter Cash's 21st Birthday Bash and Musical Bar Mitzvah. It was Sunday night, March 3, 1991. It felt like a dream.

"Hey guys," Hugh said, "at some point tonight, we will have you hop on stage and tear it up with some of your songs."

Ok, we thought, let's hope that happens *really* late after everyone has had a few drinks so the band's punk style doesn't get any of these Tennessee boys too riled up.

Most of the party was an endless parade of different musicians and singers, climbing on stage in various groupings to play spontaneous songs, jams, and surprises for John Carter. As the night wore on, Johnny's publicist came back to check on us and told us June was feeling a little under the weather and Johnny was going to drive her home. He invited us to follow him outside so we could meet the two of them before they left.

When we approached the couple in the moonlight, Johnny was in all black (of course) and June was in a print dress; her eyes did look a little tired. They made us feel so warm and welcome. They were real. Johnny shook our hands and looked us right in the eye. Kosher was able to tell him how much he loved Johnny's recent book, *Man in White*, a historical novel on the life of St. Paul. He thanked us for coming out and told us he really had hoped to be able to come by the studio to sing on the band's new record, but with his Mama's cancer battle, he had been spending day and night at her side. We told him we understood and thanked him for even considering the idea and told him that just his interest in the band had been so affirming.

We said our goodbyes. As they drove away, we just laughed and high-fived, wondering how we could have been so lucky to have had such a lovely conversation with Mr. and Mrs. Johnny Cash.

Five months earlier, I had begun work on a long-shot telephone campaign with Lou Robin, Johnny's manager, to see if Johnny would consider singing a duet with One Bad Pig on a cover of his trademark song, "Man in Black." I had suggested the song to the band for their upcoming album. As a personal challenge, I told them I would get Johnny to sing on their record. They laughed. What a joke!

I will never forget the phone call when Lou said Johnny had listened to the One Bad Pig records I mailed, and he liked what they were doing. Johnny was intrigued with the idea of supporting a punk band with a Christian message, and he was honored that they were interested in him. What? Honored? The Cash team saw this as a possible step toward validating Johnny with a fresh, young audience. In that call, Lou also revealed some of the doubts and hurts Cash was currently experiencing in his career. Five years earlier, in 1986, Columbia Records, his record label home for 28 years, had unceremoniously dropped him from their roster. The Nashville music establishment and country radio had been ignoring him and treating him like old news. Sadly, it seemed like Cash may have been questioning his artistic relevance, perhaps drifting a bit. He had been forgotten.

That was hard to imagine. For some reason, Cash's enormous worldwide, genre-smashing musical legacy, which is so clear to all of us 25 years later, was elusive in 1991. It was still two years before U2 called him to sing on their multi-platinum *Zooropa* album and rap/hard rock guru, Rick Rubin, invited him to be on his American Recordings label. With Rubin's blessing and production touch, Cash became hip again and went on to record six critically-acclaimed, commercially successful albums (his final four studio records and two posthumous album releases) that strongly cemented Cash's towering legacy for all time, across all ages.

When I told the band about that phone call with his manager, I don't believe they ever really believed the duet recording might happen or that they would even actually meet Johnny Cash.

Outside the party, as the Cash's drove away, I said, "I told you! What do you say now?"

Kosher said, "It doesn't even matter that he won't get to sing on our record, just meeting Johnny Cash tonight is something we will never forget!"

The band and I went back to work on their record the next morning. We were floating off the high from the night before. The band had five days of recording left. We would go our separate ways on Saturday, the band back to Texas and I would go home to Los Angeles. On Thursday, I got a phone call from Hugh; in spite of Johnny's mother's dire condition, he was going to try really hard to come down and record with One Bad Pig before we left town. Unbelievable! We crossed our fingers and booked Quad Studio (where Neil Young recorded the *Harvest* album) for the next day and waited. Friday morning, we watched and waited. This was our very last day in Nashville. Finally, Hugh called late that morning and said indeed Johnny would be coming; he would be there in ten minutes.

I stood on the Quad Studio outdoor back deck waiting until Johnny pulled up the gravel driveway in his black Mercedes. I walked him inside to greet the band. He was tired, but happy to be there. He had come directly from his mother's bedside to the studio. He explained that she was on her deathbed, and it was good to get away from the daily deathwatch to be with us.

According to Steve Turner's biography, "Cash's mother, Carrie, had been the single biggest influence on his life. She had not only encouraged his music and taught him about Christian faith—both through her Bible reading and the example of her life—but she had convinced Cash that his voice was a gift from God. She lived to see her son survive all the calamities [of his life] and emerge as one of the best-known Christian laymen in America. Cash, for his part, never forgot the debt he owed his mother. He knew that the best part of himself came from fulfilling the vision she'd had back in post-war (Arkansas), when she told him that God's hand was on him and that he had a special task to carry out. So convinced was he of her vision that it kept him going during the darkest days of his life. From the bowels of the Nickajack Caves where he contemplated suicide, to the bed in intensive care after his double-bypass operation in December 1988, the same thought stayed with him: 'I can't die yet because God has more for me to do.'"[3]

Before he sang that morning, he and I chatted a bit about his health. He was vulnerable about the demons he had been facing down. In the past two years, Johnny had experienced that rough double-bypass heart surgery; he was hospitalized several times with painful, life-threatening respiratory conditions; and, he had suffered a painful abscessed tooth that led to a cyst and eventually a broken jaw that left him with ongoing excruciating pain and some disfiguring of his jawline. He was sensitive about his appearance and just mad about his desire for painkillers. He acknowledged he had come too far from drug addiction to still have to deal with this level of pain; it was daily and unrelenting.

We watched him through the studio glass window plant his feet wide, stand confidently at the microphone, and begin to sing just as he had done for 37 years since that historic audition with Sam Phillips at Sun Records. His fatigue vanished. He slyly smiled and put his whole body into his performance, kicking one of his legs with emphasis as he leaned into the mic. Did he just get airborne? We all had big grins and shook our heads in disbelief. When we listened to the playback of the recording with Johnny, he asked to "hear a little more treble."

Once the recording was finished, we wandered into the big wood-paneled recording room for a group photo with Johnny and One Bad Pig. Smiles all around. There were no walls. The band was so grateful, and they genuinely expressed it. The tremendous weight of Johnny's mother's impending death, his debilitating physical pain, and his musical identity questions, had all magically evaporated from his mind and shoulders for a few moments that morning.

Before he left, someone in the band asked if we could pray for his mother and Johnny's health. With his stature as a celebrity, the offer to pray felt slightly risky and presumptuous. "Please, thank you," he said. The four punk rockers and I circled around him, laid our hands on him and prayed for comfort, strength and peace during these difficult last days for his mother and for long life and health for him. As we surrounded him with love and fervent prayer, I watched tears trickle down his face from his closed eyes. I was so thankful we offered.

Three days later, on Monday, March 11, 1991, Johnny's mother, Carrie, died at the age of eighty-six. It was a bitter blow for Cash, who cried publicly for the first time that anyone could remember.

✝ ✝ ✝

You may ask yourself, who am I? I am young, inexperienced, technically at this point in life, I'm a nobody. I don't think I have much or anything to offer when I meet someone with experience, success or accomplishments. Maybe I should simply fade into the background and watch from a distance. Just stay out of the way on the sidelines. Wrong!

What we fail to see is that the celebrity or wealthy business person or accomplished entrepreneur that we meet is often confronting the same fears, disappointments and pain that we all face. Who would have thought four young men in a barely-known Christian punk band from Texas could surround a giant like Cash who has sold 90 million records, and through their interest, affirmation and prayer bring him hope and encouragement in the midst of such a crushing transitional season?

When we made our initial inquiries, we had no idea all of the difficulties he was facing. We did not know Johnny's story.

But God knew. He saw how our days in Nashville were meant to unfold and how the members of One Bad Pig were going to be able to serve Johnny Cash with prayer, gratitude, genuine interest and affirmation.

SERVING HEALS PAIN & LOSS

Everybody hurts.

✝ ✝ ✝

Over the years, I have had the good fortune to have many seasoned mentors and leaders with wealth and experience gladly speak into my life and career. As a young businessperson, you want to make certain these interactions occur through a heart of serving, with gratitude. Don't just focus on your need for a job or a referral. Focus on the person you are meeting. Go into that conversation prepared to affirm them in their success and accomplishments. Go in as a passionate learner about their experience, ideas and approaches to business. Go in having prayed for them and their family. If it seems appropriate, you might have the opportunity to pray with them during your interaction. Pray for them after your meeting.

I can tell you from my personal experience, when you approach leaders with gratitude, genuine interest and affirmation, they walk away feeling loved and affirmed by you and the Spirit of God living in you. And, because of the seed-planting spiritual principle, very often they will naturally desire to pour into you more often and serve you more sacrificially as their protégé.

As one who now functions as a mentor to so many young people, I can tell you how much my heart shifts and changes toward those who approach our times together with a heart of serving me, or my wife, or my children. I have many young, creative clients who really can't afford to pay my legal fees at this point in their career. I still try to serve them as much as I can. But, when they are genuinely interested in serving me and my family, when they affirm me or pray for us, and they express genuine gratitude, I can't tell you how much I want to do for them over and over, with or without a legal fee.

✝ ✝ ✝

A few years ago, I spotted John Prine, one of my all-time favorite singer-songwriters, walking out of a movie theater in Nashville. My heart was racing. I have such an appreciation for his songwriting, and there are significant moments in Carol and my life where his music has been a strengthening soundtrack that I can still replay in my mind. (Plus, in that moment, it was hard not to forget my foot-in-the-mouth moment when I found myself years earlier standing next to Bruce Springsteen in a deserted Tower Records store in Hollywood at midnight. Bruce wanted to chat with me and no words would come out of my stunned mouth). In that moment, I thought, I don't want to bother John Prine during his personal time, but Lord, is there any way I should quickly serve him? I approached him, not simply as a fan, but with a desire to give to him instead of just taking.

"Mr. Prine, I just want to tell you how much your songwriting has meant to my life. I am so grateful for your creative work all of these years." He shook my hand.

He beamed. "What's your name?"

I told him.

"Well, Mark, thank you so much for saying so. That really means a lot."

✝ ✝ ✝

As an entertainment attorney in Nashville, I often find myself stuck in very difficult contract negotiations with Los Angeles or New York City-based lawyers. In my world, I do think there are some unspoken biases against being based in Nashville or the South. I am fine with that. I may not have their experience or earn what they earn, but I am confident in God's calling on my life. Sometimes those negotiations hit an unresolvable impasse, start getting heated, or turn personal, and occasionally I have experienced flagrant dishonesty from that opposing attorney. For whatever reason, when our negotiations start going off-the-rails like that, I get extremely stressed and intimidated.

God has taught me over the years to respond by serving, not by throwing more heat on the fire or by putting on the boxing gloves. First, I need to see the other attorney through God's eyes and heart. Maybe he is facing enormous pressures in his marriage. Maybe the pressures of law firm life are causing him to spin out of control. Maybe he doesn't know Christ so his eternal destiny and hope for the future is nonexistent, which is often the case. God wants me to respond to them with compassion and genuine interest. God wants me to invest time praying for their marriages, their businesses and their salvation, especially when they have no idea I'm doing so. With compassion, genuine interest, and prayer, intimidation evaporates. Then, when my heart changes toward them, their heart changes toward me, and the log jam is almost always removed—immediately. It's amazing. Walls crumble!

In the midst of difficult conflicts with others, I encourage you to believe that your genuine concern and prayer for them will supernaturally change the atmosphere.

SERVING ERASES CONFLICT

When your work is done with care,
compassion, and humility, conflict evaporates.

✛ ✛ ✛

Once a year, I have an esteemed entertainment industry business manager/ accountant named Lou speak at one of my Belmont classes. She is a firecracker. She is also a bold woman of faith. Her husband is a pastor. Lou has an office in Nashville and one in Beverly Hills, each with about 35 accountants helping to operate her business. All are Christians. She splits her time by spending every other week in each office. She handles all the accounting and business planning for high-profile, world-class music celebrities, actors and athletes like Britney Spears, Jennifer Lopez, Steven Tyler, Meghan Trainor, Florida Georgia Line and Allyson Felix. She is responsible for millions of dollars. And her success is conditioned on trust.

I asked Lou to tell my students how her faith informs her daily work. She gave several examples where she served specific clients one-on-one in personal ways that were well beyond her work for them as their accountant.

Then she began to talk about the power of consistent prayer for her clients. Every day at 11:30 a.m., all of her employees in both of her offices gather on a video conference call to discuss key issues for specific clients that day. Once they finish, they move right into prayer for all of their clients.

✢ ✢ ✢

One of the greatest ways, we can serve our friends, family, clients, business associates, and leaders is through prayer, whether we pray with them in the same room or from a distance. It's always an important way to serve, especially when you think you have nothing to give. Prayer, genuine interest, and affirmation with gratitude are mighty equalizers that are almost always welcomed and received by all, even by someone who towers over you in success, wealth and accomplishments.

CHAPTER 11:
THE GREAT ESCAPE

Strange, isn't it? Each man's life touches so many other lives.
When he isn't around he leaves an awful hole, doesn't he?
— Clarence the Angel (It's A Wonderful Life)

"Love"
— John Lennon[1]

For Carol and me, the new millennium began with us doing a circus high-wire act. Everything in our lives seemed at risk, and God kept raising the wire higher and higher while asking us to walk shoulder-to-shoulder with a number of chairs balanced on my chin and the top chair careening on one leg, holding our daughter, Sophia, and our unborn son, Harrison.

I was transitioning out of my V.P. role at a record label and was looking for an in-house legal affairs position at a new entertainment company. Nothing was available. Carol, Pastor Dale, and a few others strongly encouraged me to start my own solo entertainment law practice. That was crazy! My own business? No, no, no, I needed a steady paycheck. I was $150,000 in debt from law school tuition and we now had zero in savings, too. We had a two-year-old and one on the way. We prayed and sensed God's peace and affirmation. With no seed or start-up money, in blind faith, I opened the doors of my law office, believing new clients would somehow find me that first month. I got a call the first week and have had business every day since.

Simultaneously, we were trying to buy our very first home without me having any employment history as a lawyer and no money to put down. We were turned down by so many lenders, but we had a tenacious broker. God did a couple of miracles, and we suddenly were able to move from our duplex rental into our first home!

At the same time, Carol was pregnant with Harrison. In my job transition, there was a COBRA snafu in our health care coverage. Harrison's doctor and hospital bills would not be covered! No matter, with our doctor quietly coaching me in my ear, he let me perform the entire delivery.

"Woah, he's slippery!"

"Don't *drop* him."

The nurses were wide-eyed with their surgical masks. Harrison was born healthy! We had to put $10,000 on a credit card to take him home. Take that, Dave Ramsey! Wait a second, with my catching skills, shouldn't we receive a serious discount on our bill?

It was a perfect storm. But God held our hands every step of the way on that wire. He proved himself faithful over and over. With time, my Nashville law practice grew strong. God's assignment for me to be a counselor and connector of creatives seemed sure.

But, a few years later, I hit one of those hard walls of financial fear. (For those in your own business, you know what I'm talking about. For those starting your own business, get ready). I really could see no way out. I was losing hope and perspective. During those months, I had a dear friend reconnect me with an entrepreneur who had big dreams for building a whole new kind of entertainment company in downtown Seattle. Both were successful men with great talent and character. We began to throw around ideas about vision and staffing for the company. We talked about living spaces for my family and education plans for my children. We began to discuss a sizeable salary for me.

A couple of months later they flew me into Seattle, put me up in the W Hotel, and wined and dined me for four nights. I returned to Nashville feeling hopeful that this new opportunity was the solution to the financial pressures in our home and my law practice. This would change everything. After all, I was never that comfortable with the idea of not being on someone else's paycheck. Carol was optimistic. Leaving Nashville would be hard, but the financial relief would be worth it. I was expecting to receive their formal offer in the next few weeks.

Meanwhile, we took Pastor Dale and his wife, Joan, to see Harry Connick Jr.'s big band Christmas concert at The Ryman in Nashville. Over the warm glow of the season at an Italian restaurant beforehand, I began to enthusiastically roll out all the details of my recent Seattle trip and this new opportunity. It was a big deal, and since I had always received such genuine and heartfelt support from Pastor Dale in the past, I expected nothing less. Instead, without even glancing up from his plate of lasagna, he blurted out, "I don't think God is finished with you in Nashville yet—you have more to do here," and then instantly changed the dinner conversation to another topic.

I was dumbfounded and hurt. The night went on and I let it go. I will just need to have a few more conversations with Pastor Dale. He will eventually get it. He will come around. It will be okay. During the Connick show, an audience member presented Harry with cowboy boots to honor his visit to that famous stage, and Harry tossed his self-described "metrosexual" Louis Vuitton's up in the first-row balcony to squealing fans. We finished our night on the town.

Over the coming weeks, no job offer came. In fact, I heard nothing from Seattle. Silence. Okay...maybe this will take longer than I expected. Months and months went by. I eventually heard through the grapevine that other peers I knew were chosen as executives for the new Seattle venture. That was fine. I had no hard feelings.

A couple of years went by and the Seattle company disintegrated. There was internal dissension. And a lawsuit. What a mess. Boy, was I thankful I did not uproot my family for a move to the Pacific Northwest. God knew all along. And my pastor did, too. Pastor Dale had always been a trustworthy voice in my life. Privately, I was embarrassed that I ever doubted that for one second. For us to be able to serve others effectively, we must open our plans and assignments to God-chosen leaders and partners in our lives. We are not meant or made to go it alone. When God gives us assignments that are truly his plans, those leaders and partners are designed to help us steward and see the future more clearly. And similarly, when we begin to miss the mark in terms of our serving assignments, they can help us correct our aim.

In my financial weariness, I had begun to search for an escape plan. The Seattle dream became my plan and not God's dream or assignment for me. I was not staying true to God's assignment for me in Nashville—a community in which he had given me great favor, influence and purpose. God asks us to serve and embrace our assignments through difficulties, hardships and changing circumstances. Our lives are not about us, but about those God puts in our life to serve and love and impact. How quickly we can become like George Bailey, Jimmy Stewart's character in the Christmas classic film *It's A Wonderful*

Life, completely fed up with everyone and everything. Ready to sell our soul for a hollow and short-term solution. Ready to cash it in and escape our life assignments any way humanly possible. Pastor Dale says: "If you don't embrace your calling and begin to simply endure your calling, you will start looking for a way to escape your calling." Our hearts must embrace our assignments. Emotional and physical endurance alone will not be sufficient in trials.

For George Bailey, it took the Spirit of God (in the form of Clarence the Angel), along with those he loved and trusted, to get a right and proper perspective about his difficulties and ongoing assignment in Bedford Falls. That is what you and I need, too. The Proverbs say: "Where there is no wise and intelligent guidance, the people fall and go off course like a ship without a helm, but in the abundance of wise and godly counselors there is victory."

For me, there has been no greater counselor from which I have heard the voice of God than my wife, Carol. Which is how it should be. I am thankful that God blessed me with someone who desires to please him more than anything else in life. Carol is a woman of dependable character, depth and spiritual understanding. I may be the attorney, but she carries great wisdom for our family and community. She helps me see when I am wrong or when I begin to let something vital slide from the foreground. She encircles me with love and awakens my mind and heart to the distractions and tangents that would cause me to fall or to sail off course.

When I doubt my ability to carry out any of the assignments God has placed upon my life, her hand is always gently at the base of my back nudging me forward. When I question my ability to serve and perform in a given situation, she is always my greatest cheerleader, advocate and trusted confidante. Without ever doubting, she regularly and faithfully calls me out, "Mark Maxwell, it's in you!"

As a married person, your ability to successfully serve in every area of life is conditioned upon the strength of your marriage. If I want to serve my children effectively as a father, it starts with the level of effectiveness with which I am serving Carol each day. If I want to grow in my success as an attorney, my marriage to Carol must be growing ever stronger. If I want to be a valuable professor to my students, I must consistently value my wife, and she must be valuing me. If I want to make a godly difference in my community as a servant, I must be an agent of godly transformation in Carol's life first.

✛ ✛ ✛

We serve in partnerships, and we need partnerships to serve effectively. They help us to see more and go farther, accomplishing greatness. A good example is the friendship between C.S. Lewis and J.R.R. Tolkien. Tolkien's *The Lord of the Rings* trilogy has been a big part of our family's life. My mother is a passionate Tolkien fan who rereads the trilogy every year or so. And Carol and I have watched the film trilogy with our kids annually since the first holiday season they were old enough to glimpse the Ring-wraiths and Nazgul without crying. It took a few years.

The Lord of the Rings trilogy was a product of Christian community, not just Tolkien's isolated effort. In 1929, early in their friendship, Tolkien first took a risky step by showing Lewis his epic poem, "The Lay of Leithian," a mythical parable predecessor to LOTR filled with Christian imagery and invented languages that he had been working on for four years. His academic colleagues at Oxford in the 1920's would have turned up their noses at this sort of work. Lewis jumped in with praise-based critiques and meticulous notes. Tolkien rewrote and responded to Lewis' ideas, and Lewis began to take the same risks by showing his works to Tolkien. They continued to meet weekly for years. "The unpayable debt that I owe to him was not 'influence' as it is ordinarily understood, but sheer encouragement," Tolkien said of Lewis. "He was for long my only audience. Only from him did I ever get the idea that my 'stuff' could be more than a private hobby. But for his interest and unceasing eagerness for more I should never have brought [*The Lord of The Rings*] to a conclusion." [2][3][4][5][6]

Several years after those initial meetings, Tolkien introduced the atheist Lewis to Christ, a transformation that would change Lewis' literary assignments and his personal life. Since Lewis' death in 1963, his prolific writings on Christianity and theology are still widely read and studied by Christians and mainstream scholars alike.[7]

Tolkien and Lewis became two of the most popular authors of all time. Tolkien's *The Hobbit* (1937) and *The Lord of The Rings* (1954-55) and Lewis' *The Lion, The Witch and The Wardrobe* (1949)—the first of his seven *Chronicles of Narnia* books—are among the best-selling books ever, having sold more than 335 million copies. No other film series in the history of motion pictures has received the combination of commercial and critical success as *The Lord of the Rings / The Hobbit* series, with $6 billion in box receipts and 17 Academy Awards (out-distancing *Star Wars* with 10 and *Harry Potter* with zero Oscar wins).

✛ ✛ ✛

Over the years, I have learned to fully embrace God's calling and assignment for me to be an attorney. It never was my preference or plan, but that is okay. Often friends ask if I miss my earlier life and career as a creative A&R "music" guy. Of course! But, I know serving as an attorney is exactly where God has positioned me the past 18 years. But, which career have you enjoyed more? Well, honestly, if I compared the two, I can say that I probably loved 90% of my weekly work as an A&R person, but as an attorney, I would probably say I truly love only about 45% of my work week.

That is fine for me. Ultimately, my work is not about my joy and pleasure, it is about my obedience to God's assignment and serving others. As I serve others, with contentment and gratitude for God's plan and the trusted client relationships He has given me, the 55% of my work week I don't enjoy does not bother me. By serving with contentment and gratitude, it's like the Spirit of God waves a cloud over to cover that 55%; I know it's still there, but I can't see it anymore. Then I still get to experience the joy and pleasure God desires for me to experience in my serving. This is what the Bible means when it says He will give you the desires of your heart. It requires that your heart is first aligned with His heart. The serving plans and purposes He has designed for us always supersede our independent plans and dreams. Once our hearts are aligned, then our dreams align with His and there is great joy to be found, no matter how flawed or imperfect our jobs or careers or relationships might be.

It is impossible to serve others effectively without contentment and gratitude. As we are content and grateful in our serving, others become content and grateful for what they have received from us.

Recently, I was meeting with one of my students who was months away from earning his college business degree. He had been working for a while at a temporary job at an inner-city pawn shop. It paid pretty well, and he had some favor with his boss. It was a rough atmosphere, with lots of characters on both sides of the counter. He was surrounded by broken, desperate people, many of whom were addicts, and others who were dollars away from being homeless. My student was not really complaining about the atmosphere at all, and he was regularly able to be an agent of grace in the business, but I encouraged him to let his heart be freshly broken with compassion for those around him.

"Man, you must begin to see that pawn shop through God's eyes, as an incredible serving mission field for you. Students raise thousands of dollars in support to be sent to other continents to serve people in similar desperate situations. But God has seen fit to strategically drop you in a place with such great needs just a few miles from your home. Embrace this calling for as long as he has you there. Be grateful and content for such placement, and sacrifice yourself freshly to him to be used powerfully in those people's lives. As you do, you will find fresh joy, grace and compassion."

☦ ☦ ☦

In our selfishness, we are so often guilty of placing unreasonable expectations on each other. We are all guilty of failing to verbally express our gratitude to one another. Oh Lord, help us to forgive one another and do better and change. We are killing those we love with expectations and unexpressed gratitude.

But, turn the mirror on yourself for a moment. In your efforts to serve others, what happens when you receive zero gratitude, little or no response or acknowledgment of your love and sacrifice? When you are completely taken for granted? What happens when people take advantage of your servant's heart by bossing you around or belittling you? What happens when you sacrificially serve, and the person you are serving expects much, much more from you?

In other words, how do you respond when you are treated like a servant? Carol and I are learning to hold each other accountable in this area more each year. Lately, one of us will say to the other, "Can you believe after all I did for them, the person said nothing or barely said anything! Can you believe that?"

Then, the other one issues this reminder, "But, you did it to truly serve them, right? You did not do it for a flowery acknowledgement or glowing thank you, right? If it's really about them and not you, you must keep your heart humble and your mind right. We are in this together."

How am I going to respond when they treat me like a servant? To be successful servants, we must dispose of our insecurities and our need to find our identity in the recognition, approval and appreciation of others. We must learn to expect nothing in return. Paul says: "Do nothing from selfish ambition or conceit, but in humility count others more significant than yourselves. Let each of you look not only to his own interests, but also to the interests of others."[8]

How am I going to respond to those I have faithfully served when their words or actions are dishonoring, hurtful or even dumbfounding? When they turn their faces away and reject me or my love or my efforts? That is the great risk of loving and serving well. There is vulnerability that accompanies the assignment. C.S. Lewis said, "To love is to be vulnerable. Love anything and your heart will be broken. If you want to make sure of keeping it intact you must give it to no one, not even an animal. Wrap it carefully round with hobbies and little luxuries; avoid all entanglements. Lock it up safe in the casket or coffin of your selfishness. But in that casket, safe, dark, motionless, airless, it will change. It will not be broken; it will become unbreakable, impenetrable, irredeemable. To love is to be vulnerable."[9]

How do we move forward through such rejection and heartbreak? How do we avoid bitterness? How do we ever sacrificially serve with such passion again? We must learn to find our identity solely in Christ. Not in our serving. That is the only way. That is the key. We can experience fellowship in our pain with the One who experienced more rejection, disappointment and disloyalty than we can know. Henri Nouwen said, "In order to be of service to others we have to die to them, that is, we have to give up measuring our meaning and value with the yardstick of others…thus we become free to be compassionate."[10]

"When you base your worth and identity on your relationship to Christ, you are freed from the expectations of others, and that allows you to really serve them best," adds Rick Warren.[11] Similarly, when we identify with him and allow the Spirit to breathe into our broken hearts, he can supernaturally birth fresh compassion and freedom in us that is a wonder to those we serve and to the world around us.

☩ ☩ ☩

There is a great old saying I have spoken and heard others share with many young people over the years:

"Be faithful where you are planted."

So simple. But such a big key to success in life.

We must trust and embrace God's assignment, keep our hearts and minds humble and right about the assignment (even through the disappointments), and carry it out with gratitude and contentment.

That is the heart of a servant.

CHAPTER 12:

LIFE MOVES PRETTY FAST

All we have to decide is what to do
with the time that is given to us.
— Gandalf (Lord of the Rings)[1]

"Take Me Back"
— Andraé Crouch[2]

Who is the greatest songwriter of all time?

Stevie Wonder? Paul Simon? Bob Marley?

Good guesses.

Hank Williams? Chuck Berry?

Not quite.

It must be the amazing duo of John Lennon and Paul McCartney?

Close, but no cigar. Any true student of music or real critic of popular culture will agree.

It's Bob Dylan.[3]

For many, actually admitting to that fact becomes a reluctant concession or ends with a backhanded compliment.

Why?

Everyone agrees on his cultural impact and prophetic voice, but few have actually spent time listening to his music, studying his lyrics or developing a true appreciation of the force of nature of his "Bob-ness." That's too bad. Their loss.

Blonde on Blonde, Bob Dylan's acclaimed work and rock music's first double album, was his first recording in Nashville (in 1966). Most rock critics put *Blonde on Blonde* in the Top 10 albums of all time; many put it at #1. The album was created in the historic Columbia Studio A, which was recently renovated, reopened, and is now part of Belmont University. Most historians agree that the stamp Dylan put on Nashville by making his albums here from 1966-69 opened up the city as a legit place to make records for the rest of the pop music world.

With Belmont University's burgeoning songwriting and music business programs, I knew it was only fitting that the school should offer a music history/songwriting course on the Shakespeare of our generation. One of the greatest thrills of my career was Belmont's acceptance of my Bob Dylan new course proposal. While you might think of Dylan as a relic or a cultural icon of days gone by, I have college students lining up each spring trying to get into my class. Say or think what you will about the current generation of young creatives, I have seen otherwise; based upon their recognition of musical genius and respect for music history, I am filled with hope and optimism about the songs, songwriters and recording artists of our future.

To kick off the first semester the course was offered, I invited Dylan's side man and musical confidante, Al Kooper, to come to Nashville from Boston for a special campus-wide seminar event to discuss the historic Nashville recordings. In the history of popular music, Al Kooper's influence as a musician, songwriter, and producer is remarkable. He was a teenage friend of Paul Simon, signed his first music publishing deal at 14, and had a #1 hit song as he turned 21.

Although, Kooper boasts incredible credentials from his fifty-year music career, he is most famous for his work with Dylan. In June 1965, Al Kooper played the trademark organ riff on Bob Dylan's recording of "Like A Rolling Stone," #1 on *Rolling Stone* magazine's "500 Greatest Songs of all Time" list.[4] Al was in the band at Bob Dylan's controversial debut electric performance at the Newport Folk Festival in July 1965, #5 on *Rolling Stone* magazine's list of "50 Moments that Changed the History of Rock & Roll."[5] And in 1966, Al served as session leader and played organ on Dylan's landmark *Blonde on Blonde* album in Nashville.

Al went on to start Blood Sweat and Tears, a band that creatively birthed a hybrid genre that came to be known as jazz-rock. Al masterminded the classic blues recording, the *Super Session* album with Michael Bloomfield and Stephen

Stills, a record that arguably launched the whole "jam band" movement. He discovered, developed and produced Lynyrd Skynyrd's first three Southern Rock albums, including the ubiquitous tracks "Sweet Home Alabama" and "Free Bird," the spiritual soundtrack to my late 70's high school days. Al played on records and performed with The Rolling Stones, B.B. King, The Who, Jimi Hendrix, Cream, George Harrison, Tom Petty, Chuck Berry and Ray Charles—and the list goes on and on.

When it comes to rock history and influence, Al Kooper truly was Forrest Gump; he was "there" at so many significant moments, launching completely new musical genres and adding his unique gifts to enable superstars to shine even brighter.

Al nailed the Belmont seminar and razzed me pretty good while doing so (you can find it on YouTube). Over the course of four days, I ended up spending way more time with him than I would have ever dreamed. Al is a storyteller. A sharp jokester. He has seen it all. Whatever Al asks you to do, you do it—quickly, without hesitation. He kept me on edge while sharing story after story about my childhood musical heroes. I chauffeured him around Nashville for hours while he played me dozens of songs he wrote as a young man for pop stars like Gene Pitney, Johnny Thunder and Pat Boone. We camped out in his hotel room while he played me more recordings from the many curves and bends in his storied career. For a music geek like me, it was heaven. I was so honored.

As Al's last night in Nashville came, he surprised me once again by telling me to pick him up at his hotel; he and I would be having dinner with a friend of his.

"Yes, sir."

The friend canceled at the last minute, so it would be just Al and me one last time.

As I was driving into downtown, the Spirit of God said to me, "Mark, you are going to share your faith and my love with Al Kooper tonight."

"Absolutely not."

"Yes, you are. He trusts you. He likes you."

"Are you sure? I don't want to offend him or ruin our last night together."

"It will be fine; you won't."

"Well, I do really care about Al. He has become a friend."

"Right. This is all about serving him. It's not about you."

"I have no clue on how to do that. God, I'm nervous."

"Trust me."

As we began dinner, I kept replaying my conversation with God. I have never been more terrified of discussing my faith with anyone. Why was I so afraid? The story about Jesus is about life and hope. It is not a bad story. It is a good story. For me, it changed everything in my life. Al has received every bit of honor, glory, and opportunity the world can offer. He has walked with the musical heroes of our age. He has created timeless music that is still considered some of the greatest creative work in the last century. But, I could sense there were still some missing pieces for him.

He told me another detailed story about a phone conversation he had with Bob Dylan in 1965. Amazing. It was time. Where do I start? Okay, maybe I will start by asking about his childhood religious roots in New York City. Here goes.

"So, Al," I awkwardly cleared my throat. "Tell me about growing up in the Jewish temple—your bar mitzvah—what was all of that like for you?"

"Temple was never really my thing. There were no instruments allowed in the church. It never really connected for me. It was pretty dead."

"Really?"

"Do you want to know what my church is?"

"Uh, yeah, I do."

"When I was a teenager, my friends and I started going into the black Baptist churches in Harlem. That became my "church." That was real. That was *my* church."

"Interesting, tell me more."

"You see, I am really very spiritual, I'm just not religious," Al proclaimed with conviction. "The life, the emotions and the music in those Harlem churches blew my mind. It meant everything to me."

I was shocked; but thinking back on Al's musical work, it shouldn't have been that surprising.

Al went on for the next 45 minutes lecturing me on the complete history of black gospel music—the records, the artists—how much it all meant to the evolution of popular music, and how much it meant to him personally.

I blurted out, "But, what about the lyrics about Jesus? What did those mean to you, sitting in those black churches?"

"Hey! I'm spiritual, but THAT's religious!" as he leaned across the table with a sly grin.

God opened up a back-alley entrance in our dinner conversation that allowed me to discuss my faith, and somehow, he and I just kept going deeper. Surprise.

Toward the end of dinner, I had to ask, "Al, in your musical career, you have worked with everyone. Who would you say is your greatest musical hero of all time, your greatest influence?"

Instantly, "Without a doubt, my greatest hero and influence of all time is Andraé Crouch."

"Wait, Andraé?"

"Oh, yeah!" He then went on to explain in great detail why Andraé Crouch is the greatest musical genius (songwriter, producer, arranger and musician) of all time. Andraé was Al's hero!

As he went on, I was dumbfounded. I would have guessed he would have said Dylan, maybe Hendrix, Chuck Berry,

Ray Charles, or one of the Beatles. Now, don't get me wrong, Andraé Crouch is the "father of modern gospel music," but he is not someone typically mentioned in the same breath as those other music legends with whom Al had partnered.

"Al, you have recorded and performed with "everyone" who is "anyone" in your lifetime. I am sure you got a chance to work with Andraé along the way."

"Nope, never did."

"Wow."

"But," he said, as his eyes lit up, "I did get to see Andraé and The Disciples (his band) play a couple of times in the early 70's. Oh, they were amazing."

"Well, I guess you did get to meet him at one of those shows."

"No," as he sadly shook his head.

(When God said "Trust me," this was it.)

With goosebumps, I said, "Al, what if I told you that I was going to get you a meeting with Andraé Crouch, maybe even a phone meeting with him in the next few days?"

"Get out of here…wait…really? No way."

"Yep. My cousin is close friends with Andraé. It WILL happen. I would love to make that happen for you."

As I drove home late that night, my head was buzzing, and my heart was beating fast. I was going to be able to serve Al Kooper. I was thrilled. I called and explained the situation to my cousin David, including God's assignment for me to share the love of God with Al.

"Would you see if Andraé would be willing to befriend Al Kooper, especially knowing the tremendous impact he has had on Al's life and career? And would Andraé be willing to pick up the torch and continue sharing the love of God with my new friend?"

Exactly one week later, Al Kooper and Andraé Crouch shared a lengthy late-night phone call.

The next day I received a thank you note from Al:

> *"Thank you so much. You made my decade."*
> —@l k%per

"We miss many occasions for serving because we lack sensitivity and spontaneity," says Rick Warren. "Great opportunities to serve never last long. They pass quickly, sometimes never to return again; you may only get one chance to serve that person, so take advantage of the moment."[6] God proved to me that week that no one is out of God's reach. No matter their personality, status, wealth or religious beliefs. No one. There will always be a unique, divine strategy of how to share the love of God with each person, provided we are willing to simply make ourselves available in that moment.

✛ ✛ ✛

I know we all desire to build deep authentic relationships with others. That is the heart of God and the heart of serving. But to do so, we must become transparent, we must be real, we must be truthful. As a Christ-follower, our public faith should be completely natural and normal. Tim Keller says, "If you are not public with your faith. If you are not willing to identify as a Christian publicly. If you are not willing to give testimony, it's because you are hiding who you are. You're hiding your heart...You're lying about who you are. Why? Because if you're a Christian, Jesus should be central...central to how you face your problems...make your decisions...[and] set your life priorities. And, if that's the case, then testimony is nothing but natural. It's not something you say, 'Well, I guess I better start doing it.' What it means is if you're a Christian and you've got plenty of friends around you who find Christianity implausible, and you're not talking to them about your faith, you've short-circuited the normal course of a relationship. In the normal course of a relationship you become more transparent with one another over time. If you are not disarmingly and naturally talking to your friends about your faith, you're guilty of 'relationship malpractice.'"[7]

✠ ✠ ✠

A few years ago, I received a Facebook message from the brother of a close friend of mine from my high school in Texas.

His brother, Mike, had committed suicide. He had hung himself underneath an overpass in Fort Worth. I was grief-stricken. He was the second close high school friend who had taken his life in the past few years. Mike and I had been partners in crime— deep into drug abuse, flirting with all kinds of trouble. With all the stupid decisions he and I made together, for some reason I always escaped unharmed.

He was arrested for multiple DUI's. I should have been. He was arrested and did jail time for drug possession (more than once). I somehow always dodged arrest. I drunkenly drove and carried him into the emergency room after being cut up in a nightclub parking lot knife fight. I did not receive a blow or a scratch. Mike never finished high school. Somehow, I miraculously went on to complete college and law school. Mike battled depression and addiction much of his life. God rescued me in my early twenties from depression and drug and alcohol abuse. He went through several relationships while I have been married to one beautiful woman for almost thirty years. Mike had several children through multiple relationships, but was never emotionally able to really become a father. Being a father is one of my greatest joys.

I asked God, "Why?"

"Why was I rescued? Why did you rescue me? God, why did you always rescue me? Why not, Mike?"

I had not seen Mike in well over 30 years, so unfortunately, I never had an opportunity to tell him about Christ's love and how God rescued me.

As I prayed and sought God in my mourning, there was a lyric in a Lone Bellow song, "Bleeding Out," that kept bouncing around in my head. The line talked about our days being numbered.[8]

The group was drawing on an idea from scripture, one that came from the single psalm written by Moses. Moses says in Psalm 90:12: "(Lord) teach us to number our days, that we might gain a heart of wisdom."[9]

Numbering our days is about making every moment count. I certainly want to be a man with a heart of wisdom.

I felt like God was saying to me, "Unfortunately, Mark, you don't get to go back and correct your past, you don't get to return and make every conversation right, and you don't typically get to go back to try to change people or fix circumstances. So, you need to make every moment matter now. Make every conversation count. Consider every coffee or meeting with another as potentially the only window of time you might be able to share the story of Christ with them. Make each personal interaction an opportunity for that person to encounter me (God) in a powerful way."

God began to give me a sense of daily urgency for his transforming work. I held in my possession the cure for death.

Was I going to selfishly keep it buckled up in my briefcase? Or was I going to offer it to all those around me who were dying a little bit more each day?

One month later, I was with a client at a private VIP music event hosted on several yachts on the inland waterways of Fort Lauderdale. The night was getting late. I ended up leaning on the bar talking to the bartender over a Diet Coke. His name was Demetrius. He was a pretty somber fellow. A short, stout African American man with a 10-inch narrow goatee. I tried to have a light-hearted conversation with him, but did not get very far. A little slight smile but not much more. It was obvious he was carrying some baggage. As I walked back to the hotel, I heard the Lord say, "What about redeeming the time, numbering the days? You left Demetrius with nothing, you gave him nothing of significance."

"I am sorry, Lord. I failed, please forgive me."

Tomorrow would be a new day.

The next morning, I was spending some time doing my daily Bible reading from the One Year Bible Plan on the YouVersion iPhone app. The plan hits one passage from the Old and New Testaments and one passage each from the Psalms and Proverbs. If you stick to it, you will read the entire Bible through each calendar year.

It was December 7th, and the reading that morning included the brief Third Epistle of John. I encountered the twelfth verse which said: "Everyone speaks well of Demetrius, and so does the true message that he teaches. I also speak well of him, and you know what I say is true."

Oh man, how can this be? The only mention of Demetrius in the entire Bible is in this single passage. I checked.

I confidently knew right then God was going to redeem my failed opportunity with him the night before. I didn't know how. Fort Lauderdale is a big city, but I knew somehow I would find Demetrius. God was going to give me a second chance. I taxied down to the beach and spent a few hours enjoying the sun and sand and thought about it.

That afternoon, I taxied to the grounds of a music festival, a completely different location from the yacht event that night before. The minute my feet touched the grass I looked across the grounds to a beer concession tent. There was Demetrius, pouring a beer.

I had to hold myself back from sprinting right at him. I walked toward him at a good clip with my iPhone waving in my hand. He looked at me like I was a crazy person.

"Demetrius, did you know you are in the Bible? I was reading the Bible this morning and there you were, right in the New Testament. What do you know!"

"Let me see that," he said skeptically. I showed him the verse.

"I believe that just like Demetrius in the Bible, you are going to become a man who everyone speaks well of, a man of great respect and high reputation."

I began to tell him the story of my high school friend's recent suicide and Psalm 90, and my desire to have a heart of wisdom by redeeming and numbering my days.

"Demetrius, I want you to know I believe that God specifically sent me here to Fort Lauderdale to tell you how much he loves you! I know that might sound weird. But, I believe I am here for you."

His face was filled with emotion and awe, and I could tell he was holding back tears. He was cracking.

He intensely looked me square in the eye, "Who are you?"

He quietly revealed that his father, too, had recently committed suicide. It had been on the eve of a lengthy prison sentence his Dad was facing. He stared into my soul and queried, "Why are you here?"

He was a hollowed-out shell and stripped to the core from the loss of his Dad.

I went on telling him how much God loved him and how much he sympathized with his pain and understood his loss.

"Christ suffered and died for you, Demetrius, that you might truly live. He wants to give you hope!"

Demetrius finally said, "I can't talk to you anymore."

I watched him disappear into a port-a-potty. He later told me that he went in there to cry his eyes out without anyone seeing.

I flew back to Nashville the next day, and over the next two weeks, I began to text Demetrius various scriptures to encourage him. In addition to the loss of his father, he was a single dad who was also caring for his Mom. He was carrying a load.

Two weeks later I texted him: "Demetrius—I would like to introduce you to God's love through Christ. Would you be open to a phone call with me where I can pray with you to become a follower of Christ?"

His reply: "Yes, I would."

A few days before Christmas, Demetrius became a Christ-follower.

✝ ✝ ✝

There is a famous saying often attributed to St. Francis of Assisi that people often use to justify politically correct silence: "Preach the Gospel at all times, and if necessary use words." Two problems. There is no factual evidence that St. Francis ever actually made this statement, nor that he even lived it.[10] And secondly, it misrepresents Christ's parting words to his followers in the Great Commission. Words *are* necessary. We must be willing to say it, not just show it. That is what he requires. As we step out in faith to tell his story, God will meet us in the middle of our fear and awkwardness. But, we must step out. How will they hear, if we don't tell them?

Please understand, it is never my job to try to convert anyone; that is the assignment of the Holy Spirit. I don't have to make anything happen in someone else's mind or heart, or win some sort of moral or spiritual battle. My responsibility is to simply start the conversation, and humbly and lovingly tell my story and his story.

Telling others his redemption story is the ultimate act of serving. It is a marker of our true love for others.

Dietrich Bonhoeffer calls it "the most charitable and merciful act we can perform."[11]

✝ ✝ ✝

Life moves pretty fast.

God calls us to redeem the time and make every conversation count.

Do not limit your serving to your future career or ministry opportunity; it must start today with the classmate sitting next to you or the co-worker in the next cubicle.

Where are the places in life you have been assigned to serve that remain unrealized?

In a world filled with hate, division, and disconnection, serving astounds the world.

Where is your next assignment and mission field?

Who in your world needs the lifesaving knowledge and power of Christ right now?

Who are you supposed to serve today?

SERVING CHANGES THE WORLD–

because it changes others.

Self-sacrifice is the way, my way, to finding yourself, your true self. What kind of deal is it to get everything you want but lose yourself? What could you ever trade your soul for?

— Jesus Christ[12]

DISCUSSION QUESTIONS

The following questions may be useful for small group discussion and/or personal journaling:

Part One: Being Born

CHAPTER 1: KIBERA

1. Reflect on the author's reluctant assignment in the Kibera Slum in Kenya. Describe a time in your life when God asked you to go way outside your own comfort zone. How did your faith or character grow from that experience? How did that experience impact others? In hindsight, can you now see and describe a future or long-term purpose for you or for others through that experience?

2. Read and consider Matthew 18:1-7; Matthew 19:13-14; and Mark 10:13-16. What does Jesus say and feel about children? How should that inform our thinking, response and heart toward children? How should Jesus' statements impact and change the way we live?

CHAPTER 2: WATCH YOUR STEP

1. The author's first steps onto the Belmont University campus as a new college professor required a greater measure of faith in the midst of his fear and uncertainty. What are some of the differences and similarities in his two experiences (Kibera & Belmont)? Which experience do you identify with? Which would be more difficult for you? Why?

2. Read and reflect on Joshua 1:1-9. How have you typically overcome fear when stepping into a new situation or speaking in public?

3. Describe a time in your life where you have seen the supernatural power of prayer bring peace into a difficult or new situation.

4. The author states that when our work is focused on others through serving, the fear of failure is erased. He uses the example of the college classroom and the performance stage. List a few situations where you can begin to use prayer to serve others. Where can you use that serving principle to also overcome fear in your business, social or school setting?

Part Two: Defining Success and Networking

CHAPTER 3: WHY NETWORKING IS @#$%

1. Do you agree with the author's assertion that the quality of art, creativity and innovation is at risk due to the culture's exaggerated emphasis on social media networking? How have you experienced its damage on your own creativity, work quality or focus, or in what ways have you seen it negatively impact those in your circle of friends?

2. How do you personally identify with the pressure to use professional networking skills or to network through social media to achieve some level of success?

3. How do you respond to this cultural pressure? As you have "networked" in the past, do you relate to the feelings of moral impurity and personal conflict described in the book? Illustrate those responses and feelings in your own words.

4. Have you ever been "networked" or contacted by someone whose purpose was intended to use you in some way as opposed to building a real relationship? How did you feel and respond in that situation?

5. Read and reflect on Ecclesiastes 4:9-10. What truth does this teach us about collaboration? Discuss why building authentic relationships is a more desirable and satisfying approach to life.

Part Three: The Success of Christ

CHAPTER 4: IT'S NOT ABOUT YOU

1. Read and reflect on Matthew 20:20-24 and Mark 10:35-45. How does Jesus describe the path to success and greatness in life? How does his instruction compare with what the media, business and culture currently teach us about finding success?

2. Where do you need to get a fresh vision for serving others in order to find personal contentment and purpose (job, business, school, the arts, etc.)?

3. By faith, identify the "pain" or "wounds" in your own life that God may desire to use as "wisdom" and "medicine" for others. Begin to pray for it to be so and that such redemption would become a powerful part of your and his story.

4. By faith, begin to see your ability to change the world and leave a mark—one person at a time. Identify one or two people in your life where that can begin this week.

CHAPTER 5: MAUI = MADE IN THE SHADE

1. Read and reflect on Matthew Chapter 5. In the most famous speech in history, describe how Jesus redefines success.

2. How does one begin to achieve the success (or blessedness) Jesus describes?

3. What does it mean or look like to be successful (or blessed) independent of our circumstances?

4. The author states: "A Christ-follower is secure. He has found his true home. Once a Christ-follower knows his standing in heaven, he can live recklessly, generously and unselfishly." Does that describe your life? If not, how do you begin to get there?

Part Four: Trashing Your Agenda and Embracing Your Life Assignments and Mission Field

CHAPTER 6: BUILD AN ARK?!?!

1. Read and reflect on Proverbs 3:5-6. Are you able to believe and embrace the truth and wisdom of this instruction?

2. Read and enjoy Psalm 42:1-2 and Exodus 33:14-15. How is your current life of intimacy with God? Have you learned to cultivate a relationship with him where you can hear his voice for major life assignments and your daily decision-making?

3. What are some disciplines you may need to renew and fresh strategies you may need to add in order to consistently hear his voice and live your life by assignment? Identify friends or leaders in your life who can become encouragers to you in this vital area of growth and maturity.

4. Read Zechariah 4:6. Similar to the author's outlandish assignment to go to law school, when was a time in your life that required you to fully believe in the Spirit of God to accomplish it through you because it was so far beyond you?

5. Have you ever built dreams and preferences in your life that did not align with God's purposes and plans for you to serve others? Do some of those still exist today? If so, use this opportunity to repent and lay your dreams at his feet.

CHAPTER 7: FATHER'S DAY

1. Read and reflect on Luke 9:48 and on John 12:24-25. Consider the author's story about expanding the walls and definition of his home and family. How can you begin to expand the definition of "home" and "family" in your life? How can you begin to use your house in more ways to serve others? Identify one or two people in your life who might be deeply changed or redeemed by your love and service to them in this way. Pray about a specific plan, and begin to open your heart and home to new possibilities of making others feel known.

Part Five: Lessons in Serving

CHAPTER 8: "GOD, THIS WAS YOUR IDEA!"

1. Read and consider Matthew 6:27-34; Hebrews 13:5-6; and 1 Timothy 6:17-19. A key lesson in serving is found in those instructions.

2. The author states, *"God is my provider; clients, jobs and bosses are simply channels of provision."* Does that describe your viewpoint? Prayerfully consider adopting this scriptural truth as a personal core value. Without it, the fears and worries of life will tempt you to return to the selfish methods of networking.

3. What areas of your life do you need to roll off your shoulders and onto his today?

4. Read and reflect on 2 Corinthians 9:6-9. Identify one or two ways you can be more generous with your time, money and talent. Pray and prepare a generosity action plan, and believe for the birth of hope and supernatural results.

CHAPTER 9: NO STRINGS ATTACHED

1. Do you have the faith and desire to build relationships with others without strings attached?

2. Read 1 Peter 5:6-7; Galatians 6:7-10; and Luke 14:12-14. Do you believe the promise of God to provide for you as you serve and plant into the lives of others?

3. Whether you are a creative, student or business person, are you a person who gives value to others?

4. Reflect on the author's random lunch meeting story. What are some serving strategies you might pursue in the context of your business or school life?

CHAPTER 10: "HELLO, I'M JOHNNY CASH."

1. How can you begin to overcome the belief that you have little to give or offer those whose wealth, status, fame, creative gifts or intellect exceed your own?

2. Think about the author's Johnny Cash story. Identify others in your life you can serve and impact even though, in the world's eyes, they may seem above you in social status, finances or education. List some specific serving strategies.

CHAPTER 11: THE GREAT ESCAPE

1. Reflect on Philippians 2:3-4. When have you given your heart and time away to another and were later rejected or unappreciated by that person? How did you respond? How do the teachings of Christ encourage us to respond in that sort of situation?

2. Where are you currently assigned (job, organization, school, etc.) but are unable to find joy in that assignment? What needs to change in your heart and actions to experience fulfillment and joy?

3. Think about the author's story of Tolkien and C.S. Lewis. Who are the partners God has placed in your life to help you to serve and change the world? Who can you serve and strengthen in their service and work? Begin to pray and believe for divine relationships and friendships that will be revealed to you to achieve great and fulfilling purposes in the culture.

CHAPTER 12: LIFE MOVES PRETTY FAST

1. Consider Psalm 90:12 and Matthew 16:26.

2. When was the last time you shared your story with Christ or his story with a friend?

3. Are you able to naturally share your faith with others in a humble, relevant manner, or are you guilty of "politically-correct silence" and "relationship malpractice?"

4. Thoughtfully and prayerfully consider a fresh start now—moving beyond your fears and beginning to humbly engage the culture by serving and loving others with the truth of Christ that will set them free and give them life.

5. Who do you need to serve today?

NOTES

Part One: Being Born
CHAPTER 1: KIBERA

1. U2. "Where the Streets Have No Name." By Clayton, Adam; Evans, Dave; Mullen, Larry; Hewson, Paul. *The Joshua Tree*. U2. Universal Music Publishing Group, 1987.

2. For a good summary of Jesus' view of children, see Matthew 18:1-7, 19:13-14, and Mark 10:13-16 MSG

3. Matthew 9:17

CHAPTER 2: WATCH YOUR STEP

1. Joshua 1:3 ESV

2. Gungor. "Beautiful Things." By Gungor, Lisa, and Gungor, Michael. *Beautiful Things*. Gungor. Worshiptogether.com Songs, 2009.

Part Two: Defining Success and Networking
1. Lefsetz, Bob. "Billy Bob In Goliath." *The Lefsetz Letter blog*, May 27, 2017.

CHAPTER 3: WHY NETWORKING IS @#$%

1. Mayer, John. "Slow Dancing in a Burning Room." By Mayer, John. Continuum. John Mayer. Specific Harm Music, 2006.

2. Deresiewicz, William. "The Death of the Artist - and the Birth of The Creative Entrepreneur." *Atlantic Magazine*. January/February 2015.

3. Gladwell, Malcolm. *Outliers: The Story of Success*. Baker and Taylor, 2008. pp. 35-68.

4. Oldenburg, Ann. "John Mayer: Nobody on Twitter Creates 'Lasting Art,'" USA Today, October 5, 2010.

5. Lefsetz, Bob. "Why We've Got No Protest Music." *The Lefsetz Letter blog*, February 3, 2017.

6. Newport, Cal. *Deep Work*. Grand Central Publishing/Hachette Book Group, 2016. Introduction and Chapter 1.

7. Rice, Elisa. "John Mayer 2011 Clinic - Manage the Temptation to Publish Yourself." *Berklee Blogs*, July 11, 2011.

8. Casciaro, Tiziano, et. al. "The Contaminating Effects of Building Instrumental Ties: How Networking Can Make Us Feel Dirty." *Administrative Science Quarterly*, December 2014, vol. 59 no. 4, pp. 705-735.

9. Zhong, Chen-Bo, and Liljenquist, Katie. "Washing Away Your Sins: Threatened Morality and Physical Cleansing." *Science* 08 Sep 2006: Vol. 313, Issue 5792, pp. 1451-1452.

10. Nobel, Carmen. "Professional Networking Makes People Feel Dirty." *Harvard Business School, Working Knowledge*, February 9, 2015.

11. Ecclesiastes 4:9 KJV

Part Three: The Success of Christ

CHAPTER 4: IT'S NOT ABOUT YOU

1. Dylan, Bob. "Gotta Serve Somebody." By Dylan, Bob. *Slow Train Coming*. Bob Dylan. Special Rider Music, 1979

2. Naugle, David. "Introduction to the Christian Worldview." *Christian Worldview Journal*. Breakpoint, February 1, 2010.

3. Colossians 2:3 AMP

4. Willard, Dallas. "Jesus The Logician." *Christian Scholar's Review*, 1999. Vol. XXVIII, #4, p.610. Also available in *The Great Omission*, San Francisco: HarperCollins, 2006; and *Taking Every Thought Captive*, edited by Don King, Abilene Christian University Press, 2011. Colossians 2:3

5. Matthew 20:20-24; Mark 10:35-45

6. Bevere, John. Video teaching series, "Servants, Hirelings, Sons and Daughters," August 2016 www.messengerinternational.org

7. Wilkerson, Rich, Jr. "Servant Leadership Is Our Identity." Rendezvous Miami. YouTube video, April 27, 2016.

8. Hanbury, Aaron Cline. "Want to Change the Word: Seth Godin Knows How." *Relevant*. Issue 81: May/June 2016.

CHAPTER 5: MAUI = MADE IN THE SHADE

1. Morrison, Van. "These Are the Days." By Morrison, Van. *Avalon Sunset.* Van Morrison. Universal Music Publishing Group, 1989.

2. Nelson, Willie. "Uncloudy Day." By Atwood, J. K. From the film *Honeysuckle Rose.* 1979. Public Domain, 1879.

3. Laurie, Greg. "Blessed," *Harvest Christian Fellowship Devotional,* September 8, 2010.

4. Keller, Timothy. "Life in the Upside Down Kingdom." *Journal of Biblical Counseling,* Volume 17, Number 3, Spring 1999, pp. 48-53.

5. Keller, "Life in the Upside Down Kingdom," p. 48

6. Matthew 5

7. Keller, "Life in the Upside Down Kingdom," p. 50

8. Keller, Timothy. "Where We Are Going: The City and The Mission: Creating A Culture for The Common Good." Redeemer Presbyterian Church, April 3, 2016 podcast.

9. Bonhoeffer, Dietrich. *The Cost of Discipleship.* Touchstone, 1995. originally published 1937, pp.107-112.

Part Four: Trashing Your Agenda and Embracing Your Life Assignments and Mission Field

1. Proverbs 3:5-6 NKJV

CHAPTER 6: BUILD AN ARK?!?!

1. Zechariah 4:6 KJV

2. Warren, Rick. *The Purpose Driven Life; What Am I Here For?* Zondervan, 2002, p. 233.

3. Keller, Timothy. *Preaching: Communicating Faith in an Age of Skepticism,* Viking, 2015, p.139.

4. Psalm 139:16 NLT

5. Proverbs 3:5,6

6. Hayford, Jack W. *Pursuing The Will Of God: Meditations and Reflections from the Life of Abraham.* Multnomah, 1997, p. 8.

7. Foster, Richard J. Celebration of Discipline: *The Path to Spiritual Growth*. HarperCollins, 1978, p. 2.

8. Keller, *Preaching*, pp. 133-139.

9. Keller, Timothy. "An Identity That Can Handle Either Success Or Failure. " New Canaan Society, YouTube video, June 25, 2015.

10. Foster, p. 2.

11. Psalm 42:1-2 NLT

12. Foster, p. 1.

13. Foster, p. 39.

14. Kierkegaard, Soren. *Christian Discourses*, trans. Lowie, Walter. Oxford: Oxford University Press, 1940. p.324.

15. 1 Kings 19:11-13

16. Hayford, p. 151.

17. Hayford, p. 18.

18. Exodus 33:14-15 MSG NLT

19. Hayford, p. 15.

CHAPTER 7: FATHER'S DAY

1. Marley, Bob. "Redemption Song." By Hawkins, Edwin and Marley, Bob. *Uprising*. Bob Marley and the Wailers. Sony/ATV Music Publishing LLC, Universal Music Publishing Group, 1979.

2. Dylan, Bob. "Forever Young." By Dylan, Bob. *Planet Waves*. Bob Dylan. Ram's Horn Music, 1973. Renewed 2011 by Ram's Horn Music.

3. Frankl, Viktor E. *Man's Search for Meaning*. Beacon Press, 1949, p.77.

4. Brooks, David. "Humility in the Time of Me." Qideas.org, YouTube, April 14, 2014.

5. Genesis 17:5-6 NLT

6. Goff, Bob. *Love Does: Discover a Secretly Incredible Life in an Ordinary World*. Thomas Nelson, 2012, p. 8.

7. Warren, p. 129.

8. Cordeiro, Wayne. *The Dream Releasers*. Regal Books, 2002, p.137.

9. 1 John 4:18 ESV

10. Nouwen, Henri. *The Return of the Prodigal Son: A Story of Homecoming.* Doubleday, 1992, pp. 129-137.

11. Luke 9:48 MSG

12. Phillips, Donald T. *Lincoln on Leadership: Executive Strategies for Tough Times.* Warner Books, 1993, p. 13-25.

13. Goff, Bob. Twitter post on July 26, 2016.

14. John 12:24-25 MSG

Part Five: Lessons in Serving

1. Galatians 5:14 MSG

CHAPTER 8: "GOD, THIS WAS YOUR IDEA!"

1. Wonder, Stevie. "You Are the Sunshine of My Life." By Wonder, Stevie. Single. EMI Music Publishing, Sony/ATV Music Publishing LLC, Universal Music Publishing Group, 1972.

2. Springsteen, Bruce. "Thunder Road," By Springsteen, Bruce. *Born to Run.* Bruce Springsteen and the E Street Band. Sony/ATV Music Publishing LLC, Universal Music Publishing Group, Downtown Music Publishing, 1975.

3. Hebrews 13:5-6 AMP

4. Matthew 6:27-34 MSG

5. A collective paraphrase of Psalm 37:5-6 and Proverbs 16;3-4 to bring clarity to the Hebrew concept of "galal"

6. Tozer, A. W. *The Pursuit Of God.* originally published Christian Publications, 1948, Regal Books, 2013, p.65.

7. Remnick, David. "We Are Alive." *The New Yorker,* July 30, 2013.

8. Springsteen, Bruce. *Born to Run.* Simon & Schuster, 2016. Foreword pp. xii.

9. Kamp, David. "The Book of Bruce Springsteen." *Vanity Fair,* September 2016.

10. Hiatt, Brian. "True Bruce." *Rolling Stone,* October 20, 2016, p. 36.

11. Remnick, pg. 6.

12. Springsteen, p.17.
13. Philippians 4:19 MSG
14. 1 Timothy 6:17-19 MSG

CHAPTER 9: NO STRINGS ATTACHED

1. Jones, Norah. "Don't Know Why," By Harris, Jesse. *Come Away With Me*. Norah Jones. Sony/ATV Songs, LLC, Beanly Songs, 2002.
2. Rubin, Harriet. *Soloing: Realizing Your Life's Ambition*. Harper Business, 1999, p. 202.
3. Maron, Marc. WTF podcast, Interview with David Crosby, October 17, 2016.
4. Resnikoff, Paul. "Kim Kardashian Losing an Estimated $300,000 a Week On Social Media." Digital Music News, October 27, 2016.
5. Rubin, p. 201
6. Warren, p. 263.
7. Lewis, C. S. *Mere Christianity*. HarperOne, 2015, original 1943.
8. Keller, Timothy. *The Freedom of Self-Forgetfulness; The Path to True Christian Joy*. 10 Publishing, 2012.
9. 1 Peter 5:6-7 paraphrased
10. Frankl, p. 9.
11. Galatians 6:7-10 MSG (for additional context on this truth see 2 Corinthians 9:6-9 NLT)
12. Luke 14:12-14 MSG

CHAPTER 10: "HELLO, I'M JOHNNY CASH."

1. Cash, John R. "Man In Black." By Cash, John R. *Man In Black*. Johnny Cash. Song of Cash Music, 1972.
2. Prine, John. "Hello In There." By Prine, John. *John Prine*. John Prine. Sour Grapes Music, Inc./ Walden Music. Inc., 1971.
3. Turner, Steve. *The Man Called Cash: The Life, Love and Faith of an American Legend*. The John R. Cash Revocable Trust.

Published by the W Publishing Group, a division of HarperCollins
Christian Publishing, 2004, p. 119-120, 187.

CHAPTER 11: THE GREAT ESCAPE

1. Lennon, John. "Love." By Lennon, John. *John Lennon/Plastic Ono Band*. John Lennon. EMI Blackwood Music, Inc., o/b/o Lenono Music, 1970.

2. Keller, Timothy. "The Lord of The Rings and Redemptive Art." Redeemer City to City, 2010.

3. Carpenter, Humphrey. *Tolkien: A Biography*. Boston: Houghton Mifflin Company, ©1977, p. 148.

4. Shenk, Joshua Wolf. *Powers of Two: How Relationships Drive Creativity*. Houghton Mifflin Harcourt Publishing Company, 2014, p. 31, 32, 91, 92.

5. Glyer, Diana Patrick. *The Company They Keep: C.S. Lewis and J.R.R. Tolkien as Writers in Community*. Kent, Ohio: Kent State University Press, 2007, p. 5, 7,8, 48, 113-16.

6. Tolkien, J. R. R. *The Letters of J.R.R. Tolkien*. ed. Humphrey Carpenter with Christopher Tolkien, Boston: Houghton Mifflin Company, 2000, p. 362.

7. Briner, Bob. Roaring Lambs: *A Gentle Plan to Radically Change Your World*. Zondervan, 1993, p. 122.

8. Philippians 2:3-4 ESV

9. Lewis, C. S. *The Four Loves*. First Mariner Books, 2012, 1960, renewed 1988 by C.S. Lewis PTE Limited.

10. Nouwen, Henri. *The Way of The Heart; Desert Spirituality and the Contemporary Ministry*. HarperCollins, 1981, p. 35.

11. Warren, p. 266.

CHAPTER 12: LIFE MOVES PRETTY FAST

1. Tolkien, J. R. R. *Lord of the Rings: The Fellowship of the Ring*. George Allen and Unwin,1954

2. Crouch, Andraé. "Take Me Back." By Crouch, Andraé. *Take Me Back*. Andraé Crouch and the Disciples. Bud-John Songs, Inc., 1975.

3. *Rolling Stone Magazine,* "The 100 Greatest Songwriters of All Time." August 14, 2015; *LA Weekly,* "The Top 20 Singer-Songwriters of All Time," May 7, 2014; and *Paste* Magazine's "100 Best Living Songwriters," July 10, 2006.

4. *Rolling Stone Magazine,* "500 Greatest Songs of All Time," April 7, 2011.

5. *Rolling Stone Magazine,* "50 Moments that Changed the History of Rock and Roll," June 24, 2004.

6. Warren, p. 256.

7. Keller, Timothy. "Where We Are Going: The City and The Mission: Public Faith." Redeemer Presbyterian Church, March 14, 2016 podcast.

8. The Lone Bellow. "Bleeding Out," By Williams, Zachary; Elmquist, Brian; Knapp, Matt; and Peacock, Charlie. *The Lone Bellow.* The Lone Bellow. Mutual Trust and Treasure, Sony/ATV Tunes, 2013.

10. Psalm 90:12 NIV

11. Stetzer, Ed. "Preach The Gospel, and Since It's Necessary, Use Words." *Outreach Magazine,* August 5, 2015; Mark Galli, "Speak the Gospel; Use Deeds When Necessary." *Christianity Today,* May 21, 2009; Mark Galli, *Francis of Assisi and His World.* Intervarsity Press, 2003.

12. Bonhoeffer, pp. 7, 211.

13. Matthew 16:26 MSG